Simpsons™ Comics Unchained

Perennial

An Imprint of Harper Collins*Publishers*

In loving memory of Snowball I:

We hope there are no shots, no vets, and no pet carriers in Kitty Heaven.

SIMPSONS COMICS UNCHAINED

HarperCollins books may be purchased for educational, business, or sales promotional use. For information please write:
Special Markets Department
HarperCollins Publishers Inc.
10 East 53rd Street, New York, NY 10022

FIRST EDITION

ISBN 0-06000797-4

02 03 04 05 06 QWM 10 9 8 7 6 5 4 3 2 1

Publisher: MATT GROENING
Creative Director: BILL MORRISON
Managing Editor: TERRY DELEGEANE
Director of Operations: ROBERT ZAUGH
Art Director: NATHAN KANE
Production Manager: CHRISTOPHER UNGAR
HarperCollins Editors: SUSAN WEINBERG and KATE TRAVERS
Legal Guardian: SUSAN GRODE

Contributing Artists:
PETER ALEXANDER, KAREN BATES, TIM BAVINGTON, JEANNINE BLACK, SHAUN CASHMAN, TIM HARKINS, CHIA-HSIEN JASON HO, NATHAN KANE, JAMES LLOYD, BILL MORRISON, PHIL ORTIZ, JULIUS PREITE, MIKE ROTE, ERICK TRAN, CHRIS UNGAR

Contributing Writers:
IAN BOOTHBY, CHUCK DIXON, SCOTT M. GIMPLE, ROBERT L. GRAFF, MATT GROENING, STEVE LUCHSINGER, TIM MAILE, JESSE LEON MCCANN, BILL MORRISON, BILLY RUBENSTEIN, DOUG TUBER

PRINTED IN CANADA

TABLE OF CONTENTS

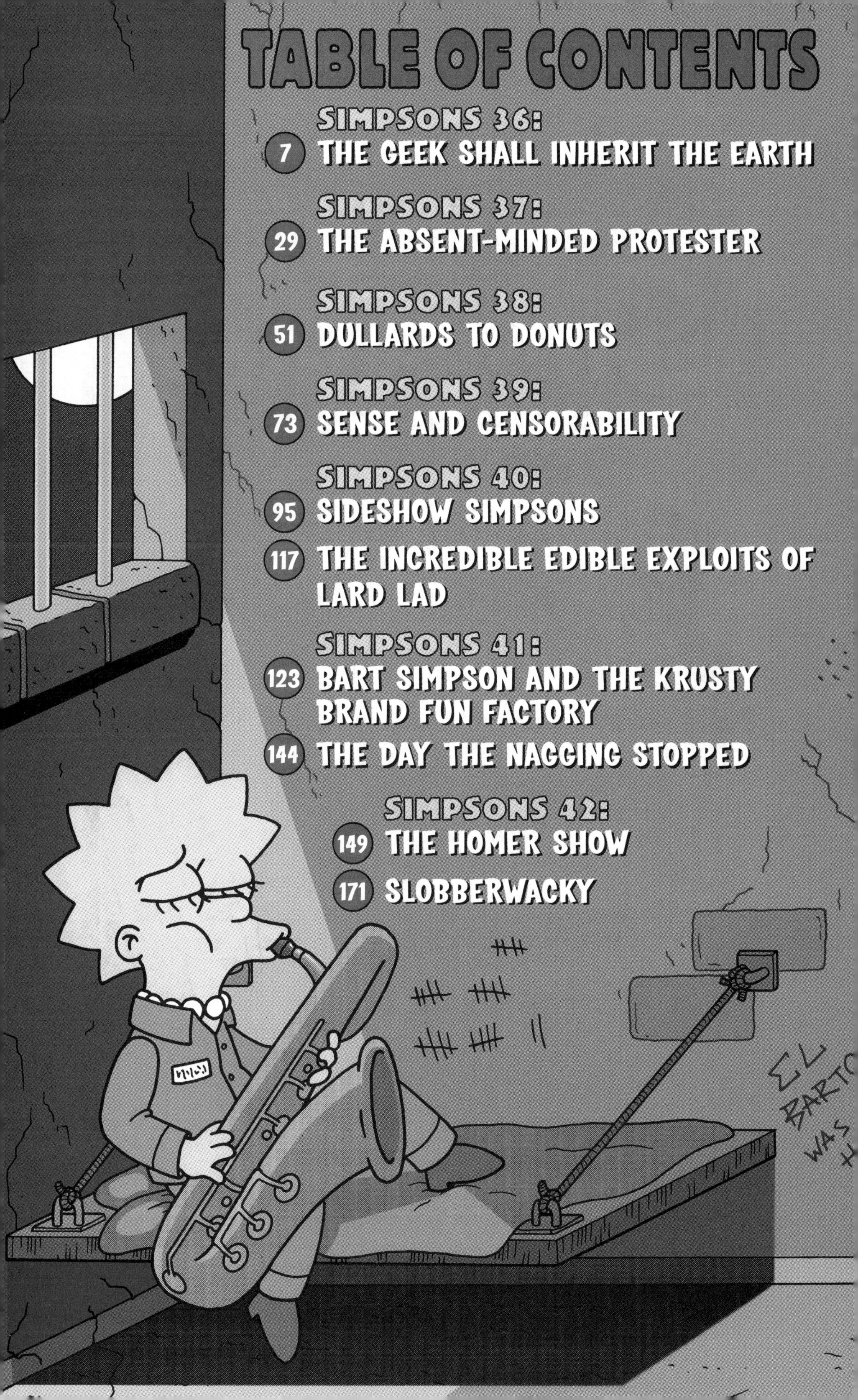

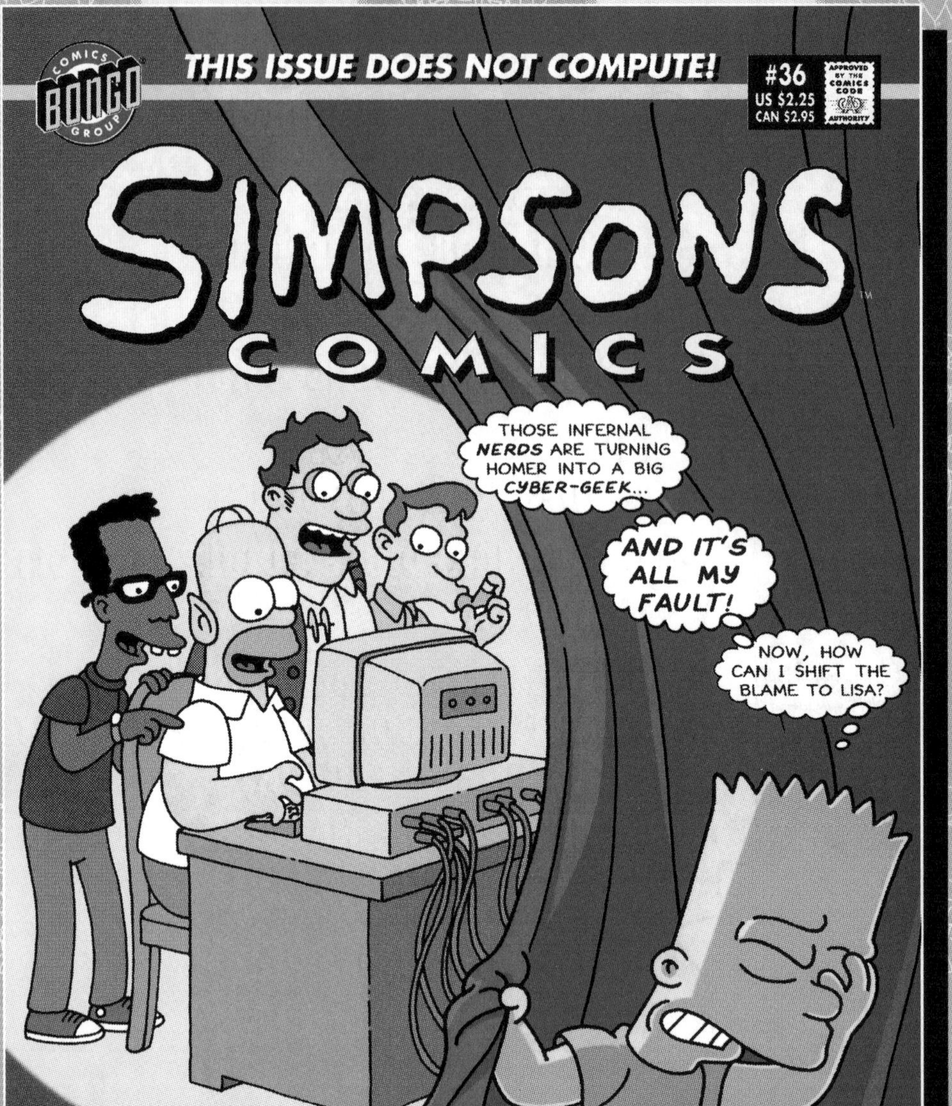
COMICS GROUP BONGO
THIS ISSUE DOES NOT COMPUTE!
#36
US $2.25
CAN $2.95
APPROVED BY THE COMICS CODE AUTHORITY
SIMPSONS
COMICS
THOSE INFERNAL NERDS ARE TURNING HOMER INTO A BIG CYBER-GEEK...
AND IT'S ALL MY FAULT!
NOW, HOW CAN I SHIFT THE BLAME TO LISA?
GROENING
©1998 BONGO ENTERTAINMENT, INC. THE SIMPSONS ©&TM TWENTIETH CENTURY FOX FILM CORPORATION. ALL RIGHTS RESERVED.

The GEEK
Shall Inherit The Earth
I CAST THEE OUT!
SCRIPT
IAN BOOTHBY
LAYOUTS
ERICK TRAN
LAYOUTS & PENCILS
JULIUS PREITE
INKS
TIM BAVINGTON
LETTERS
JEANNINE BLACK
COLORS
NATHAN KANE
REFORMED NERD
MATT GROENING

SORRY, BOYS, BUT YOU GRADUATED LAST SUMMER, AND AS THE DEAN, I HAVE TO GIVE YOUR DORM ROOM TO NEW, PAYING STUDENTS.
NOW IF YOU'LL EXCUSE ME, I'M LATE FOR THE CHARLTON HESTON FILM FESTIVAL. THE FIRST TWENTY HESTONS IN FULL COSTUME GET IN FOR HALF PRICE!
BUT... WHERE WILL WE GO? WHAT WILL WE DO?
COLLEGE WAS THE ONLY PLACE I FIT IN.
YOU MIGHT NOT BELIEVE THIS, BUT BACK IN HIGH SCHOOL I WAS A BIT OF A GEEK.
C'MON GUYS! IF SPOCK COULD COME BACK FROM THE DEAD, WE CAN DEAL WITH THIS.
YEAH, IF WE CAN FIND JOBS ON THE GENESIS PLANET.
HA!
HEE, HEE!
SNORT!
Y'KNOW, I THINK WE'RE GONNA BE ALL RIGHT.
LATER...

SPRINGFIELD NATURAL HISTORY MUSEUM
OKAY, THAT'S ENOUGH LEARNING. EITHER BUY SOMETHING AT THE GIFT SHOP OR GET OUT!
LATER, AT THE KWIK-E-MART...
HEY! THIS IS NOT A LENDING LIBRARY!
AND, AT THE LIBRARY...
HEY! THIS IS NOT THE KWIK-E-MART!
FINALLY, AT THE ANDROID'S DUNGEON COMIC BOOK EMPORIUM...
WE CLAIM SANCTUARY UNDER THE SAN DIEGO COMIC CONVENTION CODE, SUBSECTION...
YES, YES, I AM WELL AWARE OF THE TREATY. :SIGH: YOU MAY STAY IN THE BACK ROOM FOR ONE NIGHT ONLY.
YOU HAVE BEDS BACK HERE?
NO. YOU MAY SLEEP ON THE UNSOLD BOXES OF SNOWBOARDING BATMAN AND PASSIVE-AGGRESSIVE WOLVERINE ACTION FIGURES.
LATER...
Meet TV Star HENA Here Today!
ARE YOU SURE YOU DON'T WANT TO COME INSIDE, DAD? HENA, DEMOCRATICALLY ELECTED PRINCESS, REPRESENTS A FEMININE MERGING OF BOTH PHYSICAL STRENGTH AND EMOTIONAL INDEPENDENCE.
I'LL WAIT IN THE CAR, HONEY. DADDY WANTS TO LISTEN TO SPORTS ON THE RADIO.

AND NOW, HERE'S A CLIP FROM HENA'S FIRST APPEARANCE ON TROY MCCLURE'S FAILED SERIES, THE ADVENTURES OF ACHILLES.
HENA, COULD YOU GET THAT? MY FOOT'S KILLING ME!
WOW! A PLACE TO STAY AND WE GET TO MEET HENA! HER SERIES IS FANTASTIC!
EXCEPT FOR EPISODE 37.
C'MON, I THOUGHT DON KNOTTS MADE A PRETTY GOOD CENTAUR.
LOOK, IT'S URKEL!
NO... I'M NOT...
HE'S DREAMY!
GET HIM!
AND THE RED BALL FALLS IN. HE'S PULLING IT OUT. NOW HE'S SHOOTING THE PINK BALL. IT'S IN. NOW HE'S SHOOTING AT THE SAME RED BALL AGAIN...
AH, SNOOKER, MY SECRET SHAME.
BWAAAAH!
WHAT THE...

MR. SIMPSON, YOU HAVE TO HIDE US!
THEY HAD TO TAKE A BREAK, BUT WE DON'T HAVE MUCH TIME!
PUFF!
GASP!
WHEEZE!
OKAY, GET IN THE TRUNK.
ARE THE ROBOTS THAT STEAL OUR TEETH FOR THE GOVERNMENT GONE?
UM...YES.
IT'S ALL YOURS.
WELL SOD THIS FOR A KIWI'S TAIL FEATHERS. I'M OUTTA HERE!
SO A CELEBRITY LET YOU DOWN, EH? THEY'LL DO THAT. LET ME TELL YOU ABOUT THE TIME I WAS STALKING BUCK OWENS...
LATER...
THUMP! THUMP! THUMP!

JULY
MAY
JUNE
APRIL
FEBRUARY
JANUARY
LOUSY BANK CALENDARS. THE CHEAP GLUE THEY USE NEVER LASTS PAST MARCH.
RACE YOU TO THE *TV*, DAD!
AWWWWW...*PBS*? THAT'S NOT ENTERTAINMENT; IT'S *ANTI*-TAINMENT.
THEY'RE DOING A 12-PART SERIES ON HOW WE CAN PROTECT THE ENVIRONMENT.
YOU'RE IN A GOOD MOOD. NOT STILL UPSET ABOUT *HENA*?
DAD, THAT WAS ALMOST A *WEEK* AGO.
WHEN CHAINING YOURSELF TO A TREE TO PREVENT LOGGING, THE KEY IS TO CHAIN YOURSELF TO THE *TRUNK*.
THE *TRUNK* IS THE KEY. REMEMBER, *THE TRUNK!*
THE *TRUNK*? OH, *DEAR GOD,* HOW COULD I *FORGET!*
NO, MR. SIMPSON. STAMPY IS FINE. HE'S STILL VERY HAPPY HERE AT THE GAME FARM. YES...HIS TRUNK IS FINE, TOO.
WELL, *THAT'S* A RELIEF!
HEY, HOMER, I WAS GETTING THE CROWBAR OUT OF THE TRUNK. DO YOU KNOW YOU'VE GOT THREE DEHYDRATED NERDS IN THERE?

EEYEW!
GLUB!
GASP!
LATER...
I DON'T WANT THEM LIVING IN OUR HOUSE. THEY'RE DISTURBING.
BUT, MARGE, THEY DON'T TAKE UP A LOT OF ROOM, AND THEY LIVE ON KRUSTY KREAMY-OS AND BUZZ COLA. THEY'RE LIKE SEA MONKEYS BUT WITHOUT THE UPKEEP!
OKAY, OKAY, THEY CAN LIVE HERE AS LONG AS THEY STAY IN THE GARAGE.
THANKS, MRS. SIMPSON.
YOU HAVE THE WISDOM OF CAPTAIN SHERIDAN AND THE BEAUTY OF VAMPIRELLA.
THE 1970'S WARREN VAMPIRELLA. NOT THE 90'S SELL-OUT VERSION.
UMM... THANK YOU.
DAY ONE.
KLAK
KLAK
KLAK
DAY TWO.
KLAK
KLAK
KLAK

DAY THREE
THEY'RE SO BORING. THEY DON'T DO ANYTHING. JUST LIKE THOSE SEA MONKEYS.
KLAK
KLAK
KLAK
YOU GONNA FLUSH 'EM TOO, HOMER?
SON, ONE DAY YOU'LL FIND OUT THAT NOT ALL OF OUR TROUBLES CAN BE FLUSHED DOWN THE TOILET.
FOR THE RECORD, NEITHER CAN GRAPEFRUIT.
WHAT ARE YOU DOING?
OBSERVING THE NERDS IN THEIR NATURAL HABITAT AND MAKING NOTES ABOUT THEIR BEHAVIOR.
HOW JANE GOODALL. IS THIS FOR SCHOOL?
NAH, NELSON PAYS GOOD MONEY FOR ANY INFO ON NERDS. IT GIVES HIS BULLYING AN EDGE. I'M GONNA ATTEMPT INTERACTION.
IS THAT A VIDEO GAME?
YES, YOU HAVE TO SOLVE A SERIES OF INCREASINGLY DIFFICULT NEW AGE PUZZLES ON A MYSTICAL ISLAND.
WHERE'S THE VIOLENCE? IF THERE'S NO PARENT'S ADVISORY WARNING TO IGNORE THEN WHAT'S THE POINT?
WELL, WE HAVE BEEN WORKING ON SOMETHING A BIT EDGIER.
PASSWORD: FREUD!
WHOA MAMA! BUT I CAN HARDLY SEE ANYTHING WITH ALL THIS RAIN.
THAT'S YOUR ENEMY'S BLOOD.
COOOOOL! HOW DO I GET A BIGGER GUN?
OF COURSE THIS IS JUST A SMALL PART OF THE WHOLE GAME. WE NEED TO ADD THE ELVES, WIZARDS, ELABORATE CHARACTER CHARTS AND TONE DOWN THE VIOLENCE.
NEED BIGGER GUN!
KLAK
KLAK

NOOOO! YOU JUST HIT THE SEND BUTTON. THE GAME WASN'T FINISHED YET!
NOW EVERYONE WITH A MODEM HAS IT! OUR REPUTATIONS AS PROGRAMMERS ARE RUINED!
WE'RE DEADER THAN AN APPLE IIE.
WELL, I SHOULD BE GOING...NOW... SEE YA.
THE NEXT MORNING...
I'M LATE FOR WORK. NO ONE BETTER BE SLEEPING UNDER THE CAR.
HEY...WHAT'S GOING ON? KREAMY-OS WITH DOUBLE STUFF? DID YOU GUYS BECOME MILLIONAIRES OVERNIGHT?
YEP! ORDERS ARE POURING IN FOR THE FULL VERSION OF OUR NEW GAME.
WE'RE RICHER THAN DEAN HAGLUND!
KLAK
KLAK
KLAK
VIDEO GAME, EH? Y'KNOW, BACK IN HIGH SCHOOL THEY USED TO CALL ME MR. PONG!
IT'S ABOUT A GUY WHO'S A DEMONHUNTING, UNDERCOVER, MILITARY BABE-MAGNET. WE CALL IT DUMB FOR SHORT.
WHY YOU LITTLE--!
REMINDS ME OF SOMEONE.
MR. SPARKLE?
THAT'S IT!
2 3 4
5 6 7
75%
ARMOR
BULL 62 / 200
SHEL 26 / 50
ROKT 0 / 50
CELL 0 / 300

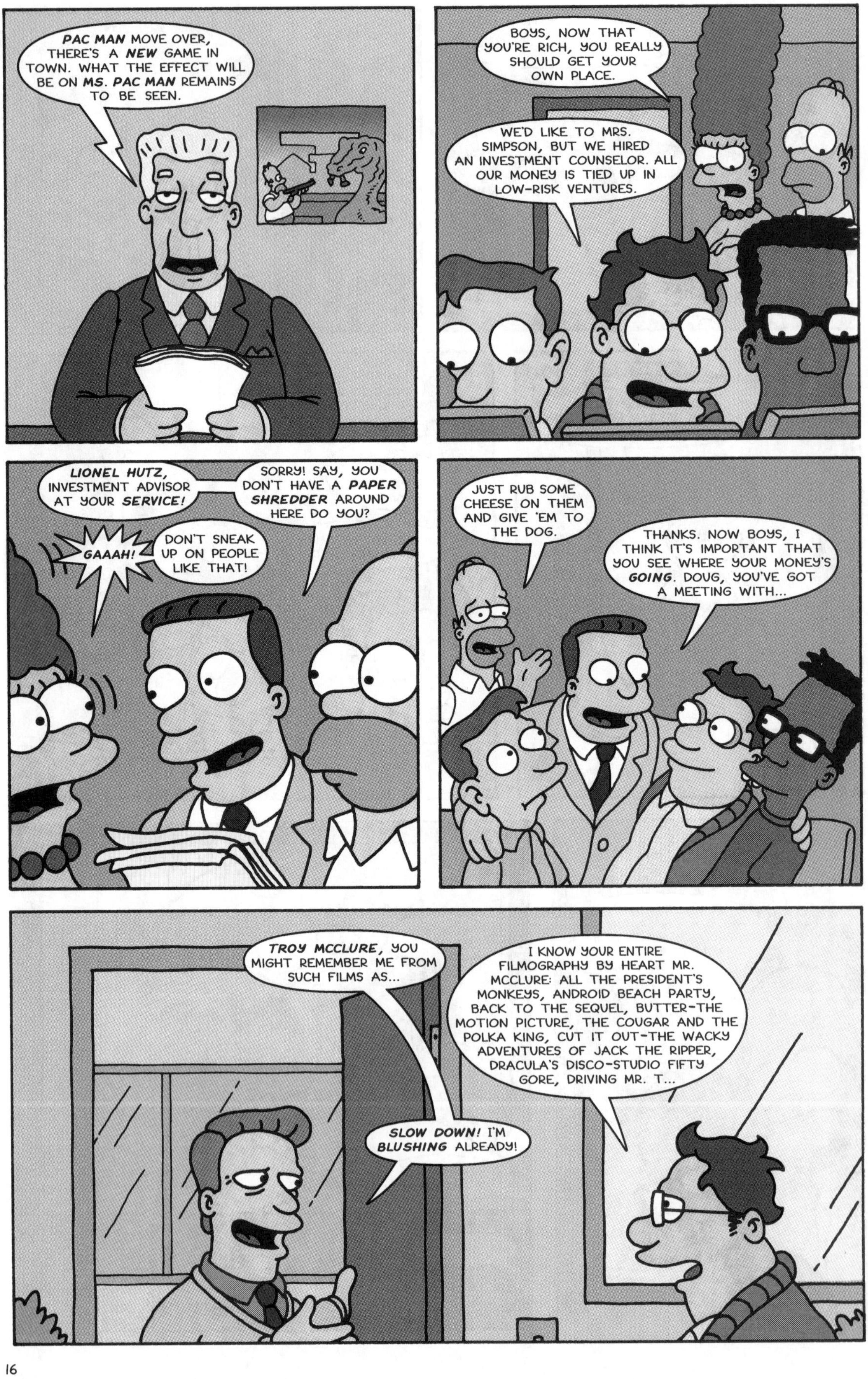
PAC MAN MOVE OVER, THERE'S A NEW GAME IN TOWN. WHAT THE EFFECT WILL BE ON MS. PAC MAN REMAINS TO BE SEEN.
BOYS, NOW THAT YOU'RE RICH, YOU REALLY SHOULD GET YOUR OWN PLACE.
WE'D LIKE TO MRS. SIMPSON, BUT WE HIRED AN INVESTMENT COUNSELOR. ALL OUR MONEY IS TIED UP IN LOW-RISK VENTURES.
LIONEL HUTZ, INVESTMENT ADVISOR AT YOUR SERVICE!
GAAAH!
DON'T SNEAK UP ON PEOPLE LIKE THAT!
SORRY! SAY, YOU DON'T HAVE A PAPER SHREDDER AROUND HERE DO YOU?
JUST RUB SOME CHEESE ON THEM AND GIVE 'EM TO THE DOG.
THANKS. NOW BOYS, I THINK IT'S IMPORTANT THAT YOU SEE WHERE YOUR MONEY'S GOING. DOUG, YOU'VE GOT A MEETING WITH...
TROY MCCLURE, YOU MIGHT REMEMBER ME FROM SUCH FILMS AS...
I KNOW YOUR ENTIRE FILMOGRAPHY BY HEART MR. MCCLURE: ALL THE PRESIDENT'S MONKEYS, ANDROID BEACH PARTY, BACK TO THE SEQUEL, BUTTER-THE MOTION PICTURE, THE COUGAR AND THE POLKA KING, CUT IT OUT-THE WACKY ADVENTURES OF JACK THE RIPPER, DRACULA'S DISCO-STUDIO FIFTY GORE, DRIVING MR. T...
SLOW DOWN! I'M BLUSHING ALREADY!

Y'KNOW, I REALLY SHOULD WRITE THAT DOWN SOME DAY, ALL THE...STUFF I DID.
YOU MEAN A RESUMÉ?
BRILLIANT! RICH AND YOU SPEAK FRENCH...
HOW I ENVY YOU!
OH MY GOSH!
YOU KNOW WILLIAM SHATNER?
KNOW HIM? HE'S MY GARDENER!
YOU WEEDS SAY YOU WANT PEACE, YET YOU... ATTACK THESE INNOCENT TULIPS. WHEN WILL YOU LEARN? WHEN WILL WE...ALL...LEARN?
ARE YOU SURE YOU DON'T WANT A MINT JULEP?
ALCOHOLIC BEVERAGES GIVE ME EYE INFECTIONS, MR. MCCLURE.
DOUGLAS, I HAVE A DREAM! A DREAM TO MAKE THE GREATEST SCI-FI EPIC OF ALL TIME! YOUR MONEY CAN MAKE THAT DREAM COME TRUE.
CAN I MAKE SURE THERE AREN'T ANY CONTINUITY ERRORS?
LIKE I SAID TO NANCY ROBERTSON IN THE 1978 CLASSIC, THREE DAMES AND A DAM, "YOU GOT IT, SUNSHINE!"
WE'LL MAKE EMPIRE STRIKES BACK LOOK LIKE RETURN OF THE JEDI!

AT THE OFFICE OF C. MONTGOMERY BURNS...
SO, GARY IS IT? I'D LIKE TO THANK YOU FOR INVESTING IN BURNS ENTERPRISES.
BUT...YOU'RE THE RICHEST MAN IN THE STATE, MR. BURNS. WHAT DID YOU DO WITH MY MONEY?
SHWUK!
I THREW IT IN THE VAULT.
DEPTH GAUGE 80ft
YES, NEPHEWS? WHAT IS IT?
THERE'S A SUNKEN GALLEON...
OFF THE COAST OF SPAIN...
THEY SAY IT'S FULL OF TREASURE!
I'M SORRY LADS. I'M BUSY WITH YOUNG GARY NOW. WE'LL HAVE THAT ADVENTURE ANOTHER TIME.
AWWWWWWWW!

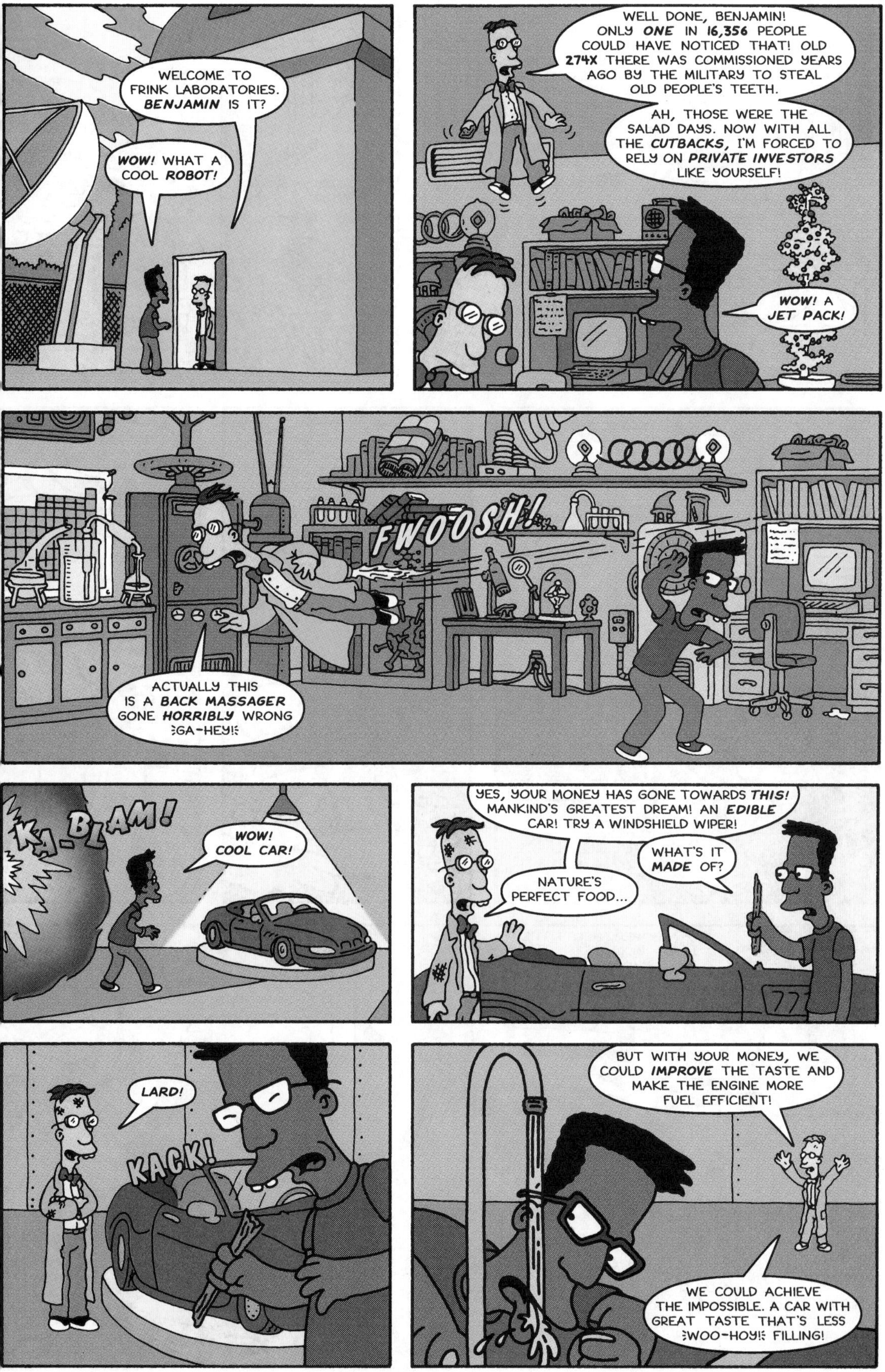
WELCOME TO FRINK LABORATORIES. BENJAMIN IS IT?
WOW! WHAT A COOL ROBOT!
WELL DONE, BENJAMIN! ONLY ONE IN 16,356 PEOPLE COULD HAVE NOTICED THAT! OLD 274X THERE WAS COMMISSIONED YEARS AGO BY THE MILITARY TO STEAL OLD PEOPLE'S TEETH.
AH, THOSE WERE THE SALAD DAYS. NOW WITH ALL THE CUTBACKS, I'M FORCED TO RELY ON PRIVATE INVESTORS LIKE YOURSELF!
WOW! A JET PACK!
FWOOSH!
ACTUALLY THIS IS A BACK MASSAGER GONE HORRIBLY WRONG GA-HEY!
KA-BLAM!
WOW! COOL CAR!
YES, YOUR MONEY HAS GONE TOWARDS THIS! MANKIND'S GREATEST DREAM! AN EDIBLE CAR! TRY A WINDSHIELD WIPER!
WHAT'S IT MADE OF?
NATURE'S PERFECT FOOD...
LARD!
KACK!
BUT WITH YOUR MONEY, WE COULD IMPROVE THE TASTE AND MAKE THE ENGINE MORE FUEL EFFICIENT!
WE COULD ACHIEVE THE IMPOSSIBLE. A CAR WITH GREAT TASTE THAT'S LESS WOO-HOO! FILLING!

DAD, YOU SHOULD BE PROUD! IT'S BEEN ALMOST THREE WEEKS SINCE THE NERDS LEFT THEIR COMPUTER COMPANY IN YOUR HANDS WHILE THEY CONTINUE TO WORK WITH TROY MCCLURE, PROFESSOR FRINK AND MR. BURNS, AND IT'S STILL A THRIVING MULTI-MILLION DOLLAR BUSINESS.
LISA, WHAT DID I TELL YOU ABOUT WORDY EXPOSITION AT THE DINNER TABLE?
RACE YOU TO THE TV, LISA?
AAAAAAAH!
TWANG!
DAD, DO YOU EVER WORRY ABOUT KARMA?
HEH, HEH!
HUH?
KARMA. REMEMBER, SIDESHOW MEL TALKED WITH FIONA APPLE ABOUT IT DURING KRUSTY'S SALUTE TO HINDUISM?
MMMMMMM... KARMA, MEL, APPLE!
ACTUALLY, BRINGING UP REINCARNATION WAS JUST A CHEAP WAY TO LEAD INTO A WEEK OF KRUSTY RERUNS.
HOMER, HERE'S THE LAST BEER IN THE HOUSE. WHOOOOOOOOAH!
NOOOOOOOOOOOOOO!

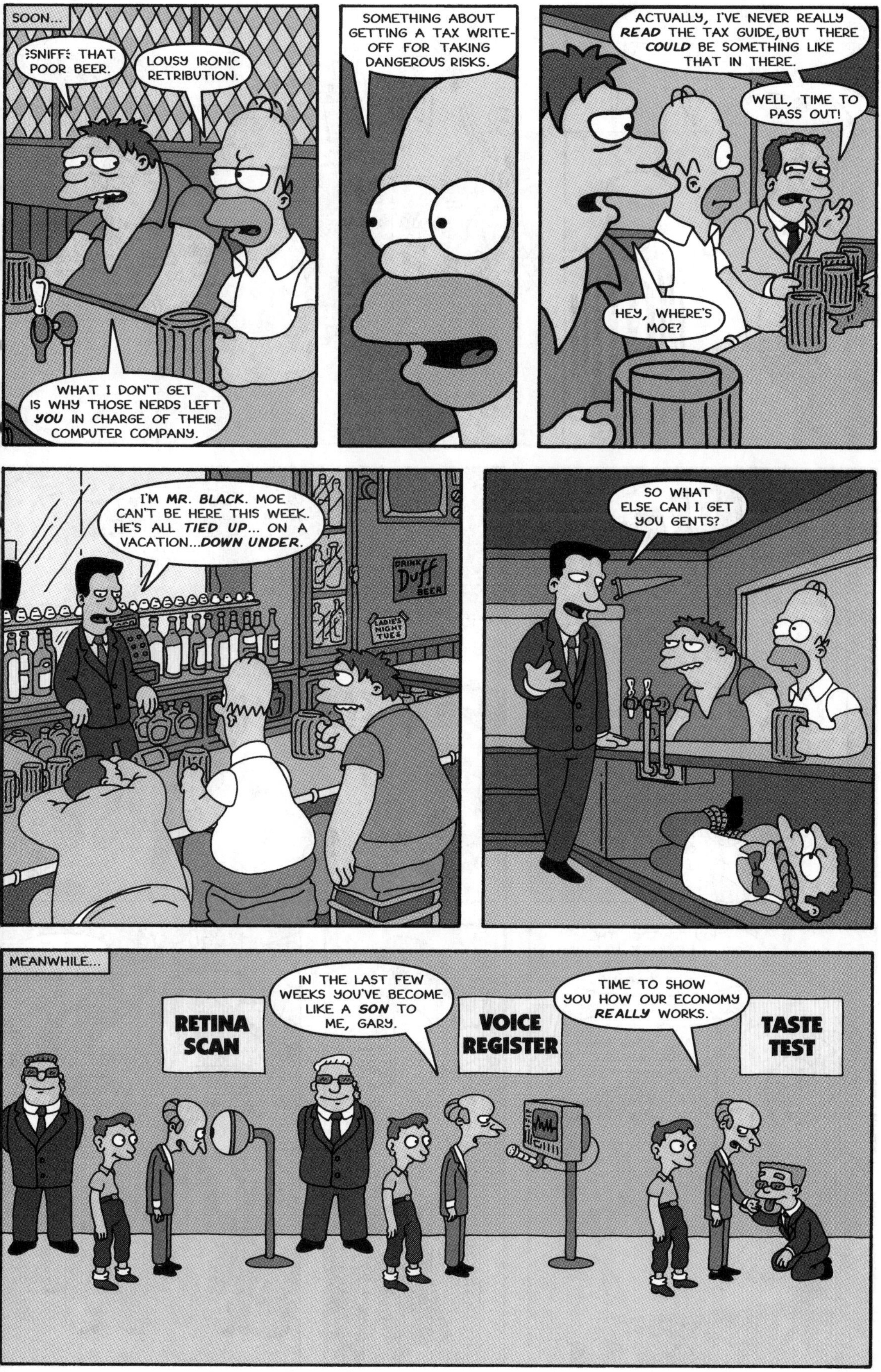
SOON...
:SNIFF: THAT POOR BEER.
LOUSY IRONIC RETRIBUTION.
WHAT I DON'T GET IS WHY THOSE NERDS LEFT YOU IN CHARGE OF THEIR COMPUTER COMPANY.
SOMETHING ABOUT GETTING A TAX WRITE-OFF FOR TAKING DANGEROUS RISKS.
ACTUALLY, I'VE NEVER REALLY READ THE TAX GUIDE, BUT THERE COULD BE SOMETHING LIKE THAT IN THERE.
WELL, TIME TO PASS OUT!
HEY, WHERE'S MOE?
I'M MR. BLACK. MOE CAN'T BE HERE THIS WEEK. HE'S ALL TIED UP... ON A VACATION...DOWN UNDER.
DRINK Duff BEER
LADIES NIGHT TUES
SO WHAT ELSE CAN I GET YOU GENTS?
MEANWHILE...
RETINA SCAN
IN THE LAST FEW WEEKS YOU'VE BECOME LIKE A SON TO ME, GARY.
VOICE REGISTER
TIME TO SHOW YOU HOW OUR ECONOMY REALLY WORKS.
TASTE TEST

THE WEASELS ARE READY MR. BURNS, SIR!
EXCELLENT!
BANG!
UP
DOWN
FINISH
DOWN IS THE WINNER BY 3 SECONDS!
DOWN
UP
DOW JONES DOWN 3 POINTS
YOU CONTROL THE *DOW JONES?* IT'S LIKE YOU HAVE THE CHEAT CODES FOR *THE ECONOMY!*
THAT'S JUST THE START. YOUR BARN DOOR IS OPEN.
ZIIIIIIP!
SMAK!
GOLD'S GONE *UP!*

YOU SEE, GARY, NO ONE REALLY UNDERSTANDS HOW THE ECONOMY WORKS, BUT NO ONE WILL ADMIT IT. ALL IT TAKES IS A FIRM HAND AND AN UNBLINKING STARE, AND THE WORLD IS YOUR OYSTER!
YOU HAVEN'T BLINKED YOUR EYES SINCE I MET YOU.
YES, BE A SPORT AND MOISTEN THEM, WOULD YOU?
ALL THAT ELUDES ME IS THE WORLD OF COMPUTERS. WITH YOUR EXPERTISE I CAN MASTER THE COMMODORE 64 AND CONQUER THE WORLD!
SpRITZ!
HOMER, YOU SEEM LIKE AN INTELLIGENT MAN, SO I'M GOING TO LEVEL WITH YOU. I REPRESENT AN EASTERN COMPUTER SOFTWARE FIRM. WE'D LIKE TO BUY YOUR COMPANY.
WHAT'S YOUR COMPANY CALLED?
"VERY COMFORTABLE SASSY PANTS AND MODEMS YES." IT DOESN'T REALLY TRANSLATE WELL INTO ENGLISH.
SORRY, NOT INTERESTED! THOSE NERDS PUT THEIR TRUST IN ME!
WELL, I HAVE A CONTRACT HERE AND I'M PREPARED TO WAIT UNTIL YOU'RE DRUNK ENOUGH TO SIGN IT!
NOT GONNA HAPPEN. I ONLY HAVE TEN BUCKS!
CONTRACT
DID I MENTION ALL BEER TONIGHT IS ON THE HOUSE?
FOR EVERYBODY?
SURE. ANY FRIEND OF HOMER IS A FAMILY MEMBER OF OURS.
ACROSS TOWN, TROY MCCLURE'S SCI-FI EPIC IS ABOUT TO PREMIERE.
AZTEC
Free Screening: Troy McClure in SATURNFORCE 3000
I READ ON FILMGORIA'S WEB PAGE THAT THEY MADE THIS IN JUST TWO WEEKS.
I HEARD THEY SHOT THE FINAL SCENE THIS MORNING.
WHERE'S THE SOUND?
TURN IT UP!

HA! HOW STUPID ARE THEY? EVERYONE KNOWS THERE'S NO SOUND IN SPACE.
LUCKY I CAUGHT THAT MISTAKE IN EDITING.
WELL, LARRY, THAT DEVOLV-O-RAY CERTAINLY DID A NUMBER ON YOU. SET A COURSE FOR THE ANDROMEDA GALAXY. WE'LL GIVE DR. NEPTUNE A TASTE OF HIS OWN SPACE MEDICINE!
C'MON! GET THERE ALREADY!
USE LIGHT SPEED OR SOMETHING!
DON'T THEY KNOW IT'S IMPOSSIBLE TO TRAVEL AS FAST AS THE SPEED OF LIGHT WITHOUT ACHIEVING INFINITE MASS AND CAUSING A BLACK HOLE? DUH!
SPEAKING OF BLACK HOLES, CHECK OUT THE AUDIENCE!
OUTSTANDING! A TRIUMPH! HUZZAH!

EXCELLENT WORK, BENJAMIN! WITH YOUR FINANCIAL AND SCIENTIFIC SUPPORT WE HAVE CREATED AN AUTOMOBILE THAT IS NOT ONLY EDIBLE BUT HAS A WINDSHIELD THAT MAKES THE DRIVER APPEAR 500 TIMES MORE HANDSOME.
Y'KNOW, I'M JUST A FIFTH-YEAR PHYSICS HONOR STUDENT BUT WHAT YOU'RE WRITING ON THE BOARD AND IN ALL YOUR NOTEBOOKS DOESN'T MAKE ANY SENSE TO ME.
GAAH! MY SCIENCE IS BASED ON FAITH RATHER THAN PHYSICAL LAWS. NOW YOU'VE QUESTIONED IT!
THE LAB IS DISINTEGRATING!
OH...SORRY.
LESS WITH THE SORRY, MORE WITH THE RUNNING!
ALL MY WORK GA-HAH! ALL MY DREAMS AH-HEY! GONE. GAH-HEY-A-HOY!
YOU'RE THE ROBOT AGAIN, AREN'T YOU?
UM, YES. THE MASTER LEFT THROUGH THE ESCAPE POD AT THE FIRST SIGN OF TROUBLE.
ON THE BRIGHT SIDE, IF YOU HAD BEEN INJURED, I WAS GIVEN INSTRUCTIONS TO KEEP YOUR BRAIN ALIVE IN THIS JAR.
OR IF THE JAR BROKE, THIS DAMP PAPER SACK.

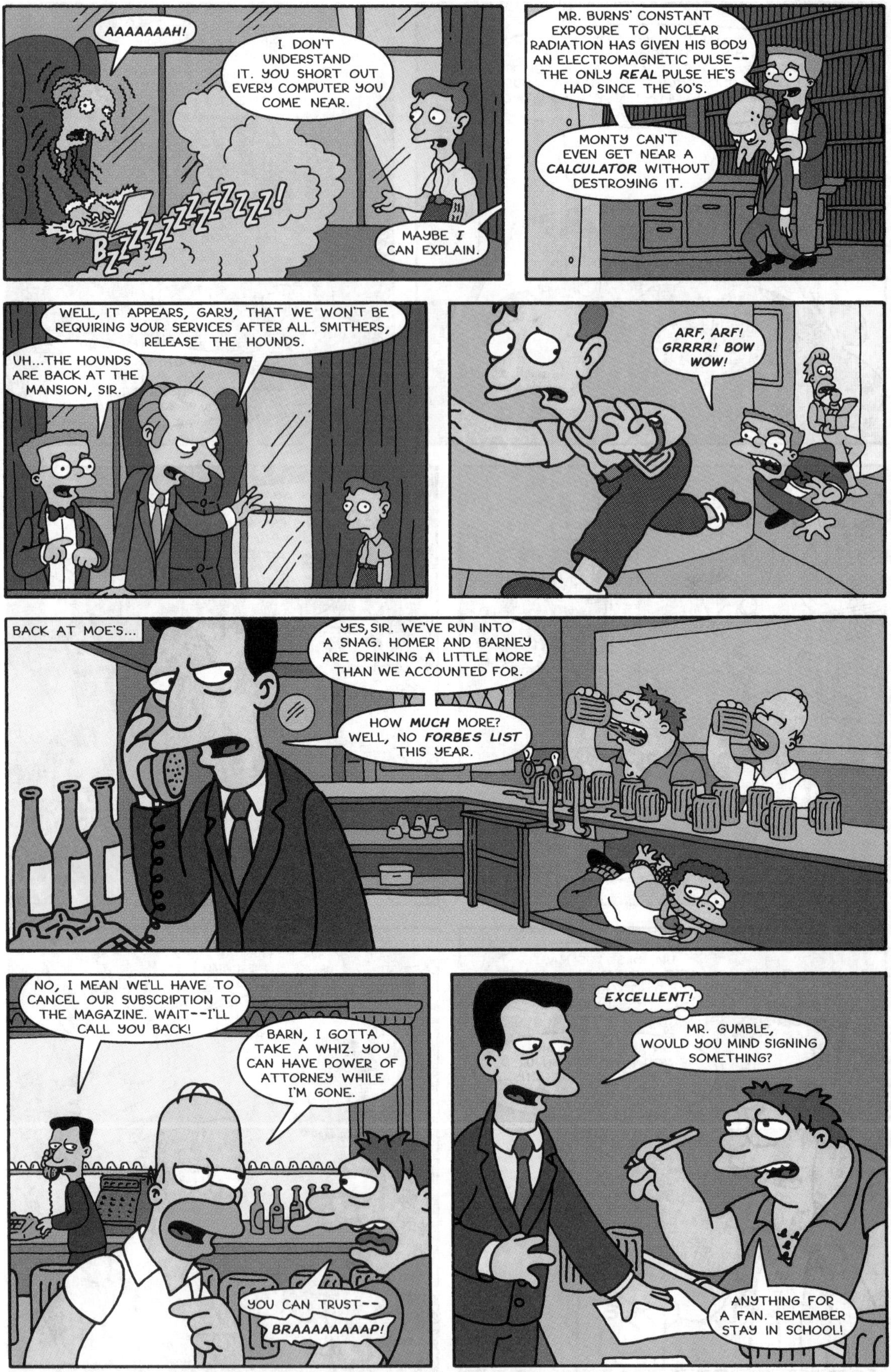
AAAAAAAH!
I DON'T UNDERSTAND IT. YOU SHORT OUT EVERY COMPUTER YOU COME NEAR.
BZZZZZZZZZZZZZ!
MAYBE I CAN EXPLAIN.
MR. BURNS' CONSTANT EXPOSURE TO NUCLEAR RADIATION HAS GIVEN HIS BODY AN ELECTROMAGNETIC PULSE-- THE ONLY REAL PULSE HE'S HAD SINCE THE 60'S.
MONTY CAN'T EVEN GET NEAR A CALCULATOR WITHOUT DESTROYING IT.
WELL, IT APPEARS, GARY, THAT WE WON'T BE REQUIRING YOUR SERVICES AFTER ALL. SMITHERS, RELEASE THE HOUNDS.
UH...THE HOUNDS ARE BACK AT THE MANSION, SIR.
ARF, ARF! GRRRR! BOW WOW!
BACK AT MOE'S...
YES, SIR. WE'VE RUN INTO A SNAG. HOMER AND BARNEY ARE DRINKING A LITTLE MORE THAN WE ACCOUNTED FOR.
HOW MUCH MORE? WELL, NO FORBES LIST THIS YEAR.
NO, I MEAN WE'LL HAVE TO CANCEL OUR SUBSCRIPTION TO THE MAGAZINE. WAIT--I'LL CALL YOU BACK!
BARN, I GOTTA TAKE A WHIZ. YOU CAN HAVE POWER OF ATTORNEY WHILE I'M GONE.
YOU CAN TRUST--
BRAAAAAAAAP!
EXCELLENT!
MR. GUMBLE, WOULD YOU MIND SIGNING SOMETHING?
ANYTHING FOR A FAN. REMEMBER STAY IN SCHOOL!

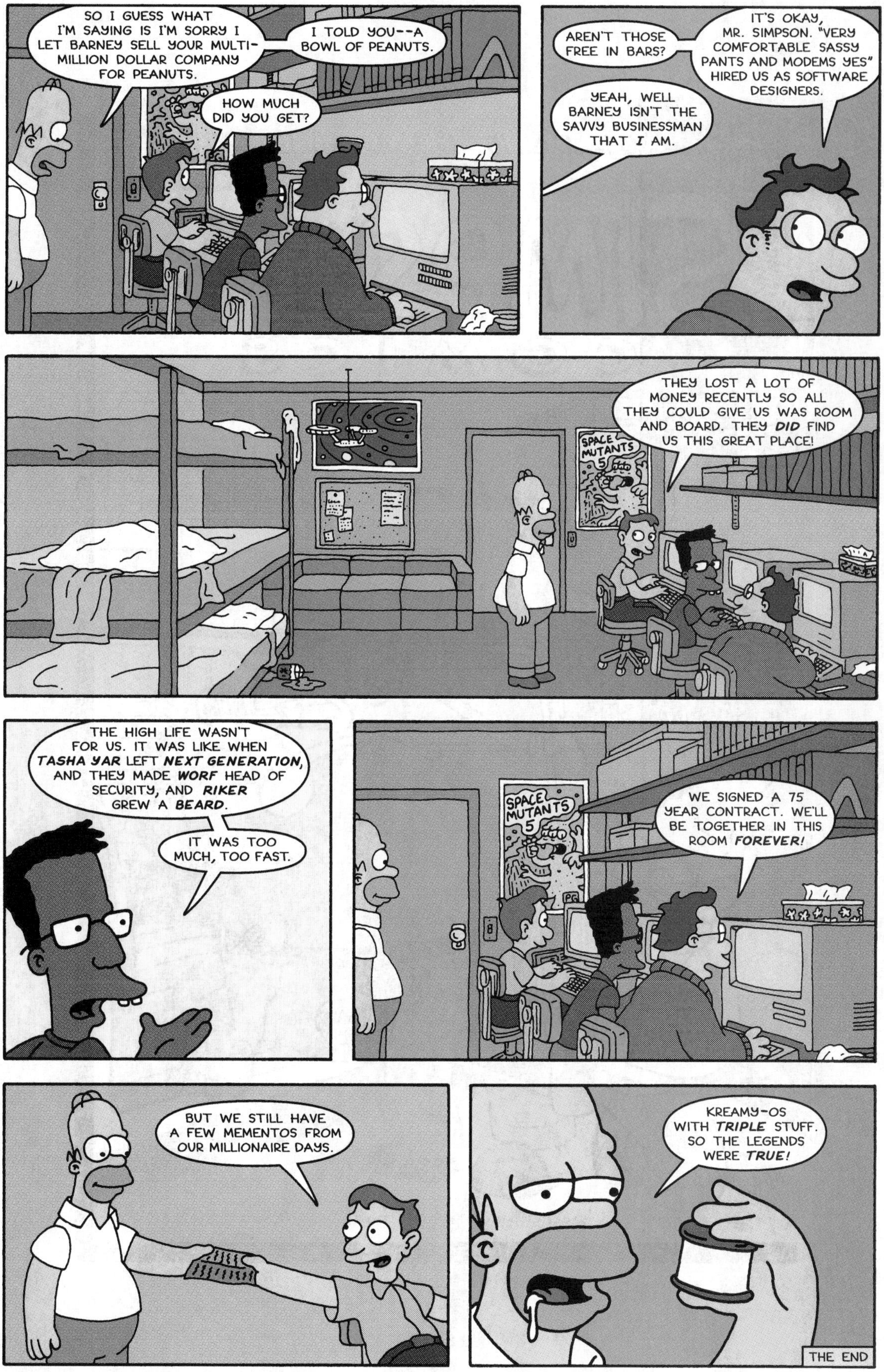
SO I GUESS WHAT I'M SAYING IS I'M SORRY I LET BARNEY SELL YOUR MULTI-MILLION DOLLAR COMPANY FOR PEANUTS.
I TOLD YOU--A BOWL OF PEANUTS.
HOW MUCH DID YOU GET?
AREN'T THOSE FREE IN BARS?
IT'S OKAY, MR. SIMPSON. "VERY COMFORTABLE SASSY PANTS AND MODEMS YES" HIRED US AS SOFTWARE DESIGNERS.
YEAH, WELL BARNEY ISN'T THE SAVVY BUSINESSMAN THAT I AM.
THEY LOST A LOT OF MONEY RECENTLY SO ALL THEY COULD GIVE US WAS ROOM AND BOARD. THEY DID FIND US THIS GREAT PLACE!
SPACE MUTANTS 5
THE HIGH LIFE WASN'T FOR US. IT WAS LIKE WHEN TASHA YAR LEFT NEXT GENERATION, AND THEY MADE WORF HEAD OF SECURITY, AND RIKER GREW A BEARD.
IT WAS TOO MUCH, TOO FAST.
SPACE MUTANTS 5
WE SIGNED A 75 YEAR CONTRACT. WE'LL BE TOGETHER IN THIS ROOM FOREVER!
BUT WE STILL HAVE A FEW MEMENTOS FROM OUR MILLIONAIRE DAYS.
KREAMY-OS WITH TRIPLE STUFF. SO THE LEGENDS WERE TRUE!
THE END

COMICS BONGO GROUP
AGE AGAINST THE MACHINE!
#37
US $2.25
CAN $2.95
APPROVED BY THE COMICS CODE AUTHORITY
SIMPSONS
COMICS
El Grampo!
El Grampo wuz Here!
WIDE LOAD
GROENING

The Absent-Minded Protester
THIS IS REALLY CREEPY, MAN!
THE STENCH OF DEATH IS EVERYWHERE...
SCRIPT
DOUG TUBER
TIM MAILE
STEVE LUCHSINGER
PENCILS
PHIL ORTIZ
INKS
TIM BAVINGTON
LETTERS
JEANNINE BLACK
COLORS
NATHAN KANE
AMERICA'S MOST WANTED
MATT GROENING

HAPPY VETERANS DAY!
...AND THE VETERAN'S DAY POT-LUCK HASN'T EVEN STARTED YET!
I HATE THIS PLACE! IT'S BORING AND GIVES ME THE WILLIES. SNIFF MMM...RUMAKI.
REMEMBER THE MAINE!
REMEMBER PEARL HARBOR!
Remember To Take Your Medicine!
OLD UNIFORM STILL FITS LIKE A GLOVE!
YOU SANK MY BATTLESHIP! BUSINESS AS USUAL, EH, FUJI?

HAPPY VETERAN'S DAY! WE MADE YOU A CAKE.
GIMME! WHAT IS THAT, CHOCOLATE? THEY RATIONED THAT DURING THE WAR. YOU DON'T WANT TO KNOW WHAT I HAD TO DO TO GET A HERSHEY BAR!

LET ME TELL YOU A LONG, LONG, LONG STORY THAT WILL PROBABLY HAVE NO POINT TO IT BY THE TIME I'M FINISHED. I WAS LIVING WITH MY PARENTS IN TRUTH OR CONSEQUENCES, NEW MEXICO, WHEN THE WAR BROKE OUT...

A SURPRISE ATTACK HAS BEEN MADE ON OUR NAVAL BASE AT PEARL HARBOR! NOW, THIS IMPORTANT MESSAGE FROM OUR SPONSOR!
FOLKS, WHEN YOU'RE FEELING RUN DOWN, THERE'S NOTHING LIKE A DOSE OF **WESTPHAL'S AUXILIATOR** TO PEP YOU UP.
NEWS OF THE WAR CHANGED MY LIFE FOREVER!
THE HORRORS OF WAR SURROUNDED ME, BUT I WAS UNFLINCHING IN MY DUTY.
THOOM! THOOM!
I NEED THOSE POTATOES PEELED BY **1700** HOURS, SWABBO. I'M ENTERTAINING LATIN BOMBSHELL ***LUPE VELEZ*** FOR DINNER.
ADMIRAL "BULL" HALSEY HIMSELF SAID MY POTATOES O'BRIEN FIRED UP THE SPIRITS OF OUR FIGHTING MEN.
AS A GREAT WAR HERO, I HAD CLOUT. I EVEN ADDRESSED CONGRESS.
WHILE THE AUTOMOBILE IS A BOON TO OUR SOCIETY, I NONETHELESS RECOMMEND THAT, BEFORE 1950, WE ENACT ***STRICT EMISSIONS CONTROLS*** AND REQUIRE ***AIR-BAGS*** IN ALL MODELS. I ALSO THINK THE FRENCH INVOLVEMENT IN VIETNAM IS A CAN OF WORMS...

THAT WAS THE FIRST TIME I WAS IGNORED...
MMM...RUMAKI. LIVER AND BACON-Y...
LETTERS TO THE EDITOR DIGEST
El Barto
AND I HAVE BEEN PERSISTENTLY AND ENERGETICALLY IGNORED RIGHT UP TO THIS VERY MOMENT.
BUT ALL THAT'S GOING TO CHANGE...
LATER THAT NIGHT...
I NEED TO DROWN MY SORROWS. GIMME A **LAWSON'S CHERRY PHOSPHATE**.
THAT IS A CONSUMER PRODUCT WHICH WE ARE IN THE PROCESS OF NOT CARRYING.
ALL RIGHT THEN, A BOX OF ***DR. GOLEM'S TAR SOAP*** AND SOME ***WESTPHAL'S AUXILIATOR***.
BY THE EIGHT ARMS OF KALI-THE-DESTROYER-OF-WORLDS, MAN, WHAT ARE YOU TALKING ABOUT?
WESTPHAL'S AUXILIATOR! I'VE WRITTEN DOZENS OF LETTERS TO YOUR PARENT COMPANY TELLING THEM TO STOCK IT! IT PROVIDES ***OOMPH*** AND A ***PEPPY OUTLOOK!***
BAM!

WELL, SIR, THAT IS YOUR PROBLEM RIGHT THERE. FOR ONE THING, NOBODY READS LETTERS ANYMORE. YOU'VE GOT TO GET *HIPPED-UP*, BY JOVE. PUT ON YOUR JAMS AND SURF...
KEEP OUT
TRY
...THE INTERNET!
www.apu.com
Click here to see my exit wound scars!
Jerkyjockey on the edge of the promised land: a Kwik-E klerk's journal
Wedding pictures:
Bouquet toss: Selma and Edna scrap for the posies.
Family friend, Homer Simpson, unconscious and bloodied.
Me carrying my wife across the threshold of the Kwik-E-Mart.
Quicktime security footage of me getting shot!
DINK!
INTERNET...BAH! I DON'T HAVE TIME FOR YOUR NEWFANGLED DOOHICKIES. I'M NOT GOING TO LISTEN TO ANY MORE OF YOUR CLAPTRAP!
BUZZ COLA
BUT MAYBE APU'S RIGHT! MY WAYS ARE AS OLD-FASHIONED AS BEARDED PRESIDENTS.
JIMBO WAS HERE
SPRAYIN
THIS
El Barto

WHY, YOU LITTLE--! DON'T PUNCTUATE ME!
PSSSST!
THAT'S IT! THAT'S HOW I'LL GET MY MESSAGE OUT! I'LL MAKE THE WORLD TREMBLE!
I DON'T REMEMBER WHERE I LIVE.

AT THE SPRINGFIELD MALL...
WITHERED THOU GOEST
Clothing for the Feeble, Infirm and Decrepit Gentleman
I NEED A VERY SPECIAL OUTFIT...
Sale!
I DON'T LIKE ANY OF THESE. I'LL COME UP WITH SOMETHING ON MY OWN.
TUG! TUG!
YANK!
BEHOLD "EL GRAMPO!" LOOK UPON ME, OH WORLD, AND DESPAIR!
STANDING UP STRAIGHT IS A DAY'S WORK. I'D BETTER TAKE A NAP.

LATER THAT DAY...
NO MORE ENSLAVEMENT TO THE INDUSTRIAL LEVIATHAN!
(AND BRING BACK WESTPHAL'S AUXILIATOR)
"El Grampo"
SPRINGFIELD MILLS DISTRIBUTION PLANT
LORDY. SOME MYSTERIOUS PERSON HAS A POTENT MESSAGE TO GET OUT. I SAY AGAIN, LORDY.
AW, CRUD-- THEY'RE ONTO US.
KRUSTY KRUNCH KORN-FLAVORED TREETZ
END BASING OF PACKAGE WEIGHT BY VOLUME! "El Grampo"
IT TOOK ME A LONG TIME TO THINK UP ALL THOSE SWEAR WORDS, AND NOW THEY'RE SPRAYED OVER. THEY'RE GONE, MAN! ALL GONE!
WE *LIVE* BY THE RATTLING CAN, WE *DIE* BY THE RATTLING CAN. THERE, THERE.
STOP TAGGERS! "El GRAMPO
NELSON RULES
JIMBO WUZ HERE
EL GRAMPO STRIKES AGAIN!
I'M TERRIBLY COLD, AND NONE OF MY VITAL ORGANS DO WHAT THEY'RE SUPPOSED TO.

THE EL GRAMPO SPREE CONTINUES UNCHECKED, A MENACE TO SOCIETY WHICH RANKS WITH JACK THE-RIPPER, AL CAPONE, THE UNABOMBER, AND SIMON BAR SINISTER, WHO, WHILE A CARTOON CHARACTER, NEVERTHELESS CAUSED UNDERDOG THE SAME LEVEL OF GRIEF WE'RE ALL SUFFERING ON A DAILY BASIS.
QUIT MAKING SUCH AN INFERNAL RACKET! ~El Grampo
EXPERTS HAVE DETERMINED THIS IS NOT THE WORK OF YOUR GARDEN-VARIETY, DISENFRANCHISED, YOUTHFUL PUNK, BUT A CALCULATING, CLEVER DEMON IN HIS GOLDEN YEARS.
I CAN'T BELIEVE THIS WANNA-BE IS GETTING SUCH GREAT PRESS! HE'S OBVIOUSLY AN AMATEUR! LOOK AT HIS TAG! HE KICKED BACKSPRAY UP ALL OVER THE FUSELAGE. AND CHECK OUT THE DRIPPAGE... AND THE LACK OF RIBALDRY!
I DON'T WISH TO SOUND INFLAMMATORY OR GO OFF HALF-COCKED, BUT THE OBVIOUS SOLUTION IS TO ROUND UP EVERYONE OVER THE AGE OF SEVENTY AND HAVE THEM PUT SWIFTLY TO DEATH!
HMMMM... I DON'T APPROVE OF A PERSON BECOMING A CELEBRITY BY DEFACING PROPERTY--I DON'T REALLY APPROVE OF CELEBRITIES, PERIOD--BUT I THINK THAT SOLUTION IS A BIT HARSH.
OH C'MON, MARGE. PUTTING HIM TO DEATH WOULD BE GOOD FOR HIM. IT WOULD GIVE HIM INCENTIVE.
GERIATRIC FREAK TERRORIZES CITY... WAIT'LL THEY GET A LOAD OF ME...

LET'S GO LIVE TO SPRINGFIELD ELEMENTARY FOR THE WIGGUM PRESS CONFERENCE, ALREADY IN PROGRESS.
WITH THE SPRINGFIELD 500 COMING UP, I JUST WANT TO SERVE NOTICE TO THIS SO-CALLED "EL GRAMPO," THAT WE WILL NOT HAVE GRAFFITI MARRING OUR BELOVED EVENT.
AND BECAUSE THE LAW-ENFORCEMENT COMMUNITY OF SPRINGFIELD IS COMPLETELY POWERLESS TO STOP HIM, WE'RE TAKING STEPS TO CLEAN UP THE TAGGING. THE FOLLOWING PARKING VIOLATION OFFENDERS ARE HEREBY PLACED ON GRAFFITI-REMOVAL DETAIL. IN ALPHABETICAL ORDER, SAMPSON, HOMER, AND SIMPSON, HOMER.
D'OH!
CORRECTION, THAT WAS A TYPO. THE TWO ON GRAFFITI-REMOVAL WILL BE SIMPSON, HOMER, AND SIMPSON, HOMER.
D'OH! D'OH!
THAT'S IT! EL GRAMPO IS AN EL HACKO! I'M ROOTIN' THIS COOT OUT!
HOW?
ELEMENTARY, MY DEAR LISA. SPRINGFIELD ELEMENTARY!
BART'S BIG BOOK OF VANDALISM

SOON...
HEY YOU KIDS, CUT THAT OUT!
—El Grampo
BULL'S-EYE!
BULL'S-EYE RED
#0294
ACME HARDWARE
LATER...
I NEED TEN CANS OF NEWCASTLE BLUE, AND TEN CANS OF BULL'S-EYE RED.
$9.99
WHAT THE--?? GEEZ, GRAMPA. LEAVE SOME FOR EL GRAMPO!
OH, BOY. OH, GOSH.
THINGA-MAJIGS! $2.69 lb
EL GRAMPO ALERT
FALSE ALARM
CALLING ALL CARS! WE HAVE AN ALARM AT 1563 ROSEMONT WAY. FOOTSPEED FOR AN AVERAGE MAN IS FIVE MILES PER HOUR. YOUR FUGITIVE'S NAME IS EL GRAMPO!

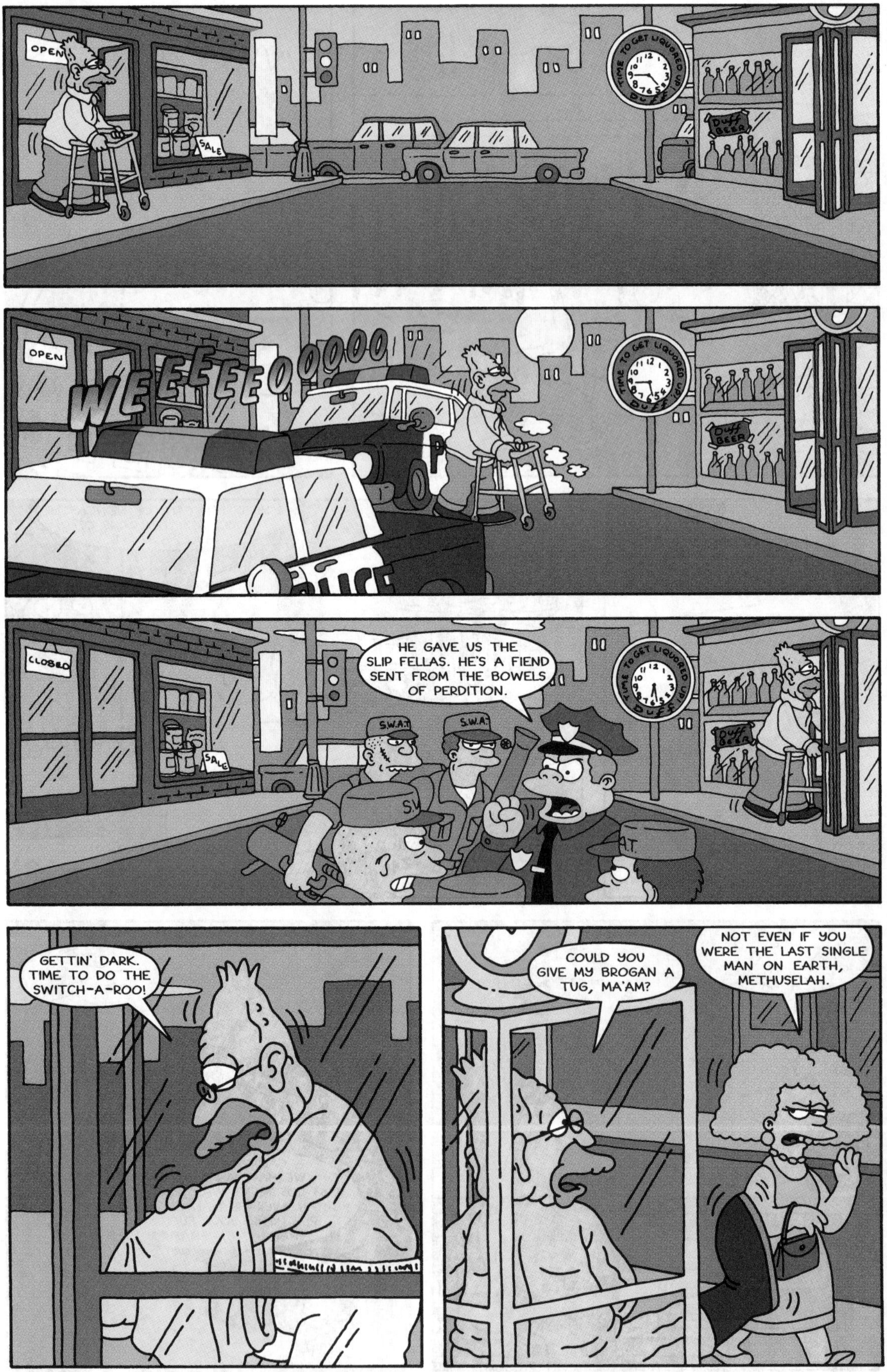
OPEN
SALE
TIME TO GET LIQUORED UP!
DUFF
Duff BEER
CLOSED
HE GAVE US THE SLIP FELLAS. HE'S A FIEND SENT FROM THE BOWELS OF PERDITION.
S.W.A.T.
GETTIN' DARK. TIME TO DO THE SWITCH-A-ROO!
COULD YOU GIVE MY BROGAN A TUG, MA'AM?
NOT EVEN IF YOU WERE THE LAST SINGLE MAN ON EARTH, METHUSELAH.

LATER...
EL GRAMPO, I PRESUME...
AGGHH! WHO'S THAT? I NEARLY SWALLOWED MY TEETH.
GRAMPA?! IS THAT YOU?
I STILL DON'T BELIEVE IT. Y... YOU KILLED THAT EL GRAMPO GUY AND STOLE HIS CLOTHES. RIGHT?
NOPE. I'M THE GENUINE ARTICLE. EL GRAMPO, IN THE PALE, BUMPY FLESH. IMPRESSED?
YOU BET I AM! NOW I KNOW WHERE I GET MY OUTLAW STREAK! CAN I GO WITH YOU?
TOO DANGEROUS, BOY. WHERE I'M GOING, YOU CAN'T FOLLOW. WHAT I'VE GOT TO DO, YOU CAN'T BE ANY PART OF.
IT DOESN'T TAKE MUCH TO SEE... THAT I'M... A HILL OF BEANS... AMOUNTING TO... I FORGOT WHAT I WAS SAYING.
BUT GRAMPA, I WANT TO GO WITH YOU, TO HELP YOU FACE THE DANGER. I LOVE YOU GRAMPA... AND IF YOU DON'T TAKE ME, I'LL RAT YOU OUT BEFORE YOU EVEN KNOW WHAT HIT YOU.
HE THREATENED TO HAVE ME PROSECUTED TO THE FULL EXTENT OF THE LAW! WHY, THAT MUST MEAN... HE RESPECTS ME!
RIGHTY-O, THEN. LET'S ROLL.
AND SO IS BORN THE MOST PROLIFIC PARTNERSHIP IN TAGGING HISTORY-- EL BARTO AND EL GRAMPO!
EL GRAMPO AND EL BARTO RULE
3407
EL GRAMPO

HEY EVERYBODY, MEET MY GRANDSON. HE'S VISITING ME, AND HE DOESN'T EVEN HAVE TO!
SURE, SIMPSON--THINK YOU'RE COCK-OF-THE-WALK BECAUSE YOU HAVE A RELATIVE WHO ISN'T PRETENDING YOU'RE DEAD. WELL, JUST WAIT TILL MY BIRTHDAY WHEN MY SON'S REALTOR SENDS ME A CALENDAR. YOU'LL WHISTLE A DIFFERENT TUNE.
HEY GRAMPA, TELL ME AGAIN HOW YOU TAGGED MAYOR QUIMBY'S HOUSE.
WASN'T QUIMBY'S HOUSE, IT WAS QUIMBY. YOU'RE KINDA INTERESTED IN MY STORIES NOW, EH, BOY?
THEY'RE WAY BETTER NOW. BEFORE, YOUR MOST EXCITING STORY WAS ABOUT WAVING AT SOME GUY NAMED ADLAI STEVENSON DURING A PARADE.
EL GRAMPO REMAINS AT LARGE, SO I'M INSTITUTING A CITY-WIDE DRAGNET TO APPREHEND THIS FUGITIVE.
I WANT A HARD-TARGET SEARCH OF EVERY DOGHOUSE, HENHOUSE, GREENHOUSE AND OUTHOUSE IN SPRINGFIELD. I PERSONALLY WILL COVER EVERY STEAKHOUSE AND HOUSE OF PANCAKES, AND ANY OTHER DINER WITH A HOMEY ATMOSPHERE, OR WHERE THE MENU PUNCHES OUT INTO A PIRATE MASK.
WIGGUM! THAT GUY COULDN'T APPREHEND A DEAD TURTLE!
LOOKS LIKE THE FUZZ IS COMING DOWN ON US. WELL, I GUESS OUR REIGN OF TERROR IS OVER. I'LL JUST GO BACK TO THE ADLAI STEVENSON STORY. HE WAS RIDING IN A '49 DESOTO. WAVED RIGHT AT ME, BIG AS DAY.
BUT GRAMPA, YOU HAVEN'T GOT YOUR WESTPHAL'S AUXILIATOR YET! I SAY WE TAKE ONE MORE SHOT AND GO OUT IN A BLAZE OF SELF-DESTRUCTIVE GLORY!
BUT IT'S TOO DANGEROUS OUT THERE. I COULD GET CAUGHT AND SPEND THE REST OF MY LIFE IN SUPERVISED CONFINEMENT.

LOCKDOWN IN FIVE MINUTES YA GREY-HAIRED GRUNTS! AND NO MORE WATER FOR MRS. GLICK!
AW, THUNDERPANTS! I WANT MY WESTPHAL'S AUXILIATOR! I SAY WE TAKE ONE MORE SHOT AND GO OUT IN A BLAZE OF SELF-DESTRUCTIVE GLORY. THAT IS, IF YOU CAN MUSTER THE GUTS, BOY!
BUT GRAMPA, I JUST SAID THA--
QUIET, I TELL YA! LET'S GET CRACKIN'! I THINK I KNOW JUST THE THING!
LATER, AT THE SPRINGFIELD INTERNATIONAL SPEEDWAY...
WELCOME TO THE SPRINGFIELD 500 AND THE THRILLING SPECTACLE OF FUEL-INJECTED ADVERTISEMENTS FOR BEER AND CIGARETTES HURTLING AT DEATH-DEFYING SPEEDS, OFFERING EAR-SPLITTING TESTAMENT TO MAN'S DESIRE TO EXCEL, AND, IF WE'RE LUCKY, A FIERY CRASH TO LIVEN THINGS UP.
LARAMIE Seniors CIGARETTES
When your next cigarette could be your last, make it a Laramie Senior!
CAN'T GET ENOUGH OF THAT WONDERFU
DON'T SHOW UP, EL GRAMPO... DON'T SHOW UP, EL GRAMPO...
BEER
GRAFFITI ERADICATOR

AH, THE DUFF BLIMP, GLIDING INTO OUR LIVES LIKE A GIANT SWAN WHO MAKES US WANT BEER.
GREAT PLAN, GRAMPA. THIS OUGHTTA GET YOU YOUR AUXILIATOR.
IT'LL DEFINITELY GET US BOTH A GREAT STORY TO REMEMBER... YOU READY?
GERONIMO!
BANZAI!

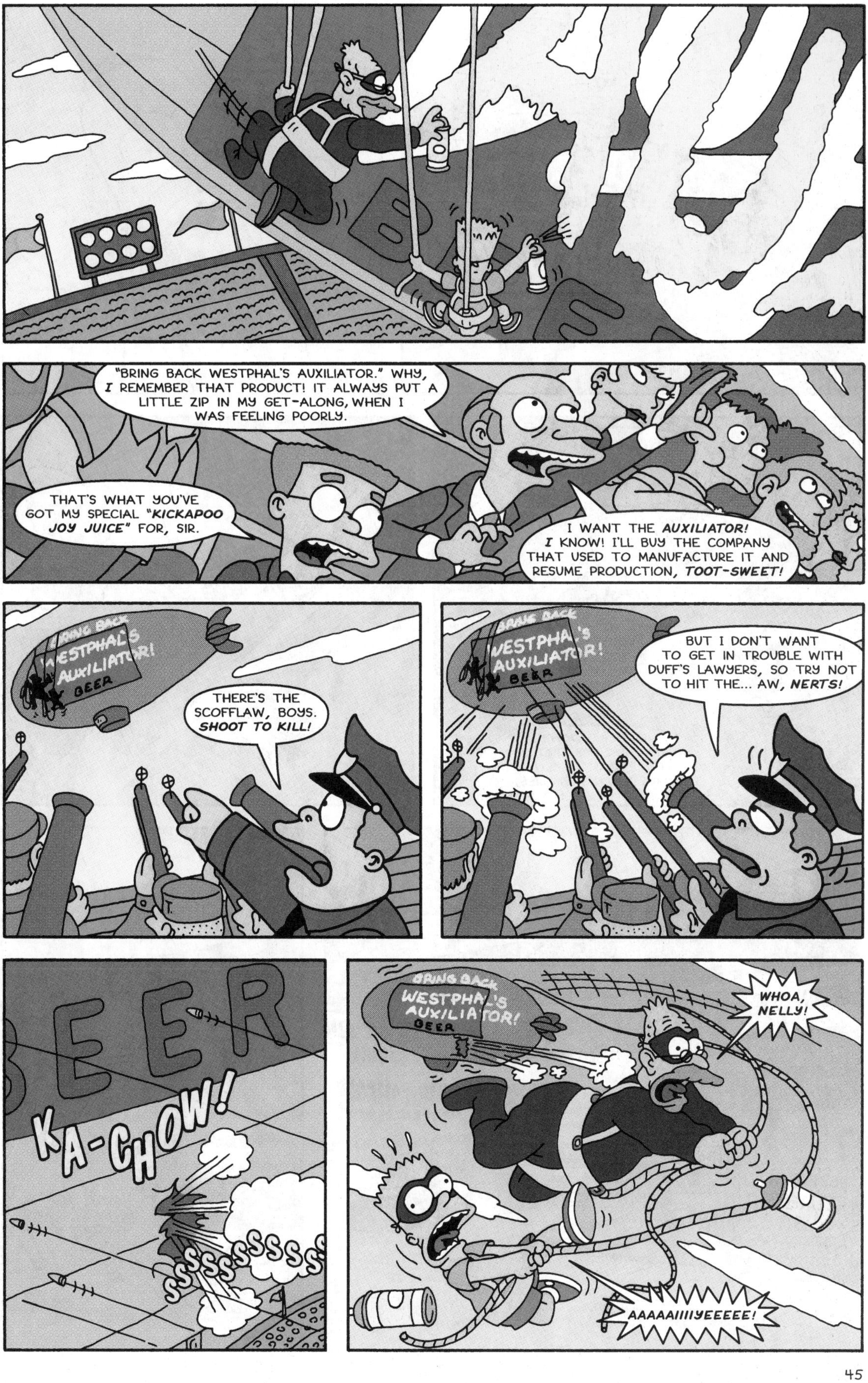
"BRING BACK WESTPHAL'S AUXILIATOR." WHY, I REMEMBER THAT PRODUCT! IT ALWAYS PUT A LITTLE ZIP IN MY GET-ALONG, WHEN I WAS FEELING POORLY.
THAT'S WHAT YOU'VE GOT MY SPECIAL "KICKAPOO JOY JUICE" FOR, SIR.
I WANT THE AUXILIATOR! I KNOW! I'LL BUY THE COMPANY THAT USED TO MANUFACTURE IT AND RESUME PRODUCTION, TOOT-SWEET!
WESTPHAL'S AUXILIATOR!
BEER
THERE'S THE SCOFFLAW, BOYS. SHOOT TO KILL!
BRING BACK WESTPHAL'S AUXILIATOR!
BEER
BUT I DON'T WANT TO GET IN TROUBLE WITH DUFF'S LAWYERS, SO TRY NOT TO HIT THE... AW, NERTS!
BEER
KA-CHOW!
SSSSSSSSS
BRING BACK WESTPHAL'S AUXILIATOR!
BEER
WHOA, NELLY!
AAAAAIIIIYEEEEE!

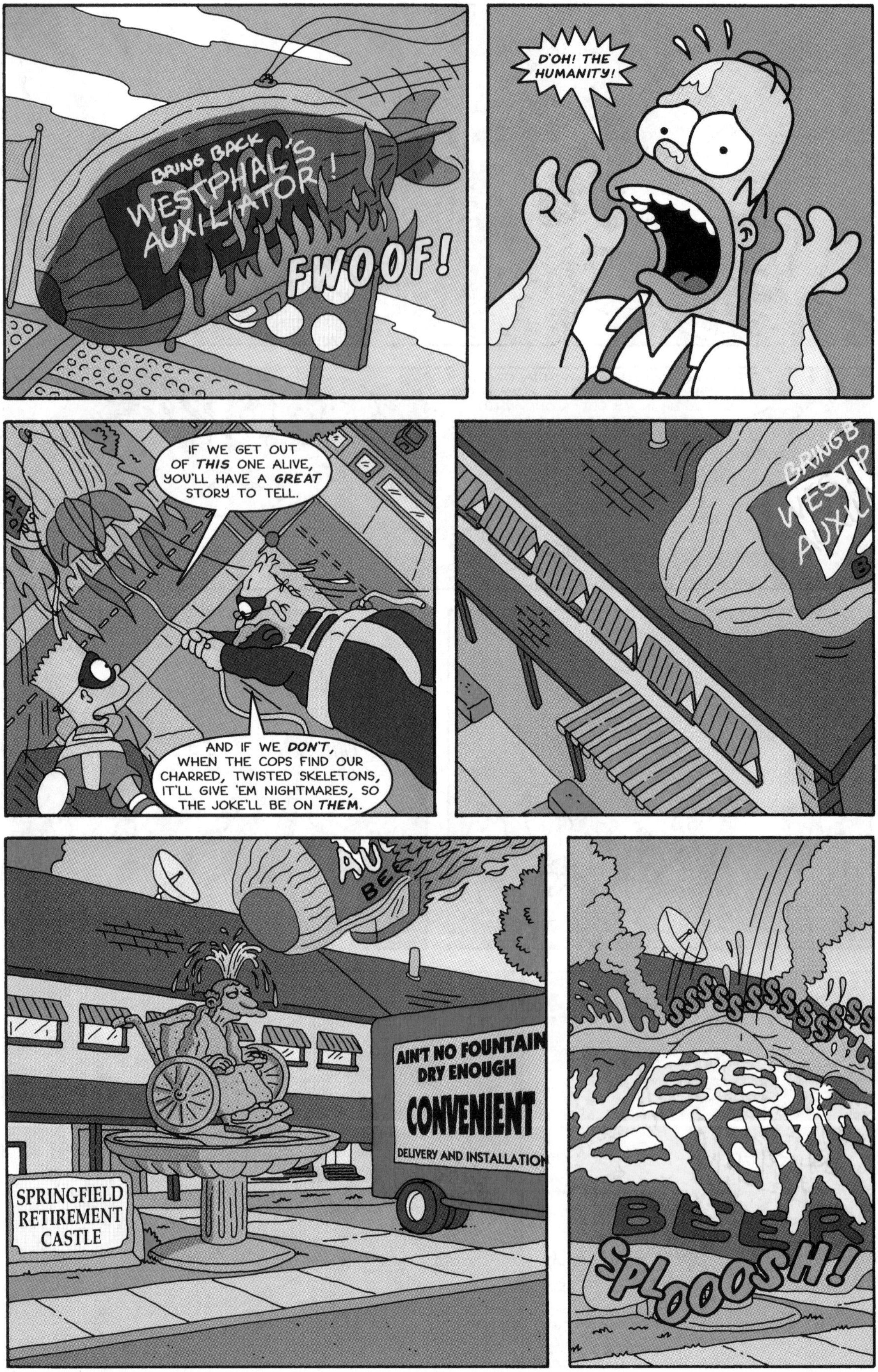
BRING BACK WESTPHAL'S AUXILIATOR!
FWOOF!
D'OH! THE HUMANITY!
IF WE GET OUT OF *THIS* ONE ALIVE, YOU'LL HAVE A *GREAT* STORY TO TELL.
AND IF WE *DON'T*, WHEN THE COPS FIND OUR CHARRED, TWISTED SKELETONS, IT'LL GIVE 'EM NIGHTMARES, SO THE JOKE'LL BE ON *THEM*.
AIN'T NO FOUNTAIN DRY ENOUGH
CONVENIENT
DELIVERY AND INSTALLATION
SPRINGFIELD RETIREMENT CASTLE
SSSSSSSSSSSSS
BEER
SPLOOOSH!

DON'T MOVE, EL GRAMPO!
SO, WE FINALLY GOT YOU. IT WAS JUST A MATTER OF TIME.
YOU CAN'T ARREST HIM. HE ONLY DID IT SO I'D PAY SOME ATTENTION TO HIM.
SAY, THAT *IS* A GOOD WAY TO GET FAMILY TO DROP BY. KIDS WORSHIP CRIMINALS.
YOU GOT THE WRONG MAN THERE, CHIEF. *I'M* EL GRAMPO!

NO, I'M EL GRAMPO!
NO, I'M EL GRAMPO!
IF IT'LL GET MY GRANDKIDS HERE, I'M EL GUAPPY!
I'M EL GRAMPO!
'TIS I THAT BE EL GRAMPO, AND FAIRLY TOLD!
CRIMINY! THEY'RE ALL EL GRAMPO! THERE'S ONLY ONE THING TO DO.
SHOOT 'EM ALL, BOYS!

...SO, WHEN ONE OF THE OTHER COPPERS TOLD WIGGY THAT HE'D HAVE TO FILL OUT A PILE OF PAPERWORK...
...HE DECIDED NOT TO SHOOT US AND INSTEAD MADE US DO BATTLE AS GERIATRIC GLADIATORS TO WIN THE TITLE OF EL GRAMPO. LUCKILY, I WON.
SO THAT'S THE STORY OF HOW YOUR GRAMPA BECAME A CARBUNKLE ON SOCIETY'S KIESTER! I CHANCED **DEATH!** I **LAUGHED** IN THE FACE OF **JOHN LAW!** I STAYED AWAKE **LOOOOONG** PAST MY BEDTIME!
PRUNE JUICE
GLUG! GLUG!
PRUNE JUICE
LARGE TEXT MAGAZINE
ALL OF IT, JUST TO STAND UP, BE COUNTED, AND STOP BEING IGNORED! IT WAS ALL WORTH--
BUH-DAH-BUP-TAH!
HERE, GRAMPA.
WESTPHAL'S AUXILIATOR! WHERE IN THE NAME OF WILFORD BRIMLEY--
THE KWIK-E MART JUST STARTED STOCKING IT. I FOUND IT IN THE POWDERED ITEMS SECTION WHERE DAD HANGS OUT.
WESTPHAL'S AUXILIATOR
THANKS, BOY. YOU KNOW, ALL THIS REMINDS ME OF WESTPHAL'S OLD SLOGAN. "IT DOESN'T MATTER IF YOU GET OLD AND ARE SUBSEQUENTLY IGNORED BY FRIENDS, LOVED ONES, AND THE GENERAL PUBLIC, YOU CAN STILL HAVE PEP WITH WESTPHAL'S!"
WELL, ENJOY.
OH, I WILL. BELIEVE ME, I **WILL!**
WHAT DID YOU GET ME AGAIN?
THE END

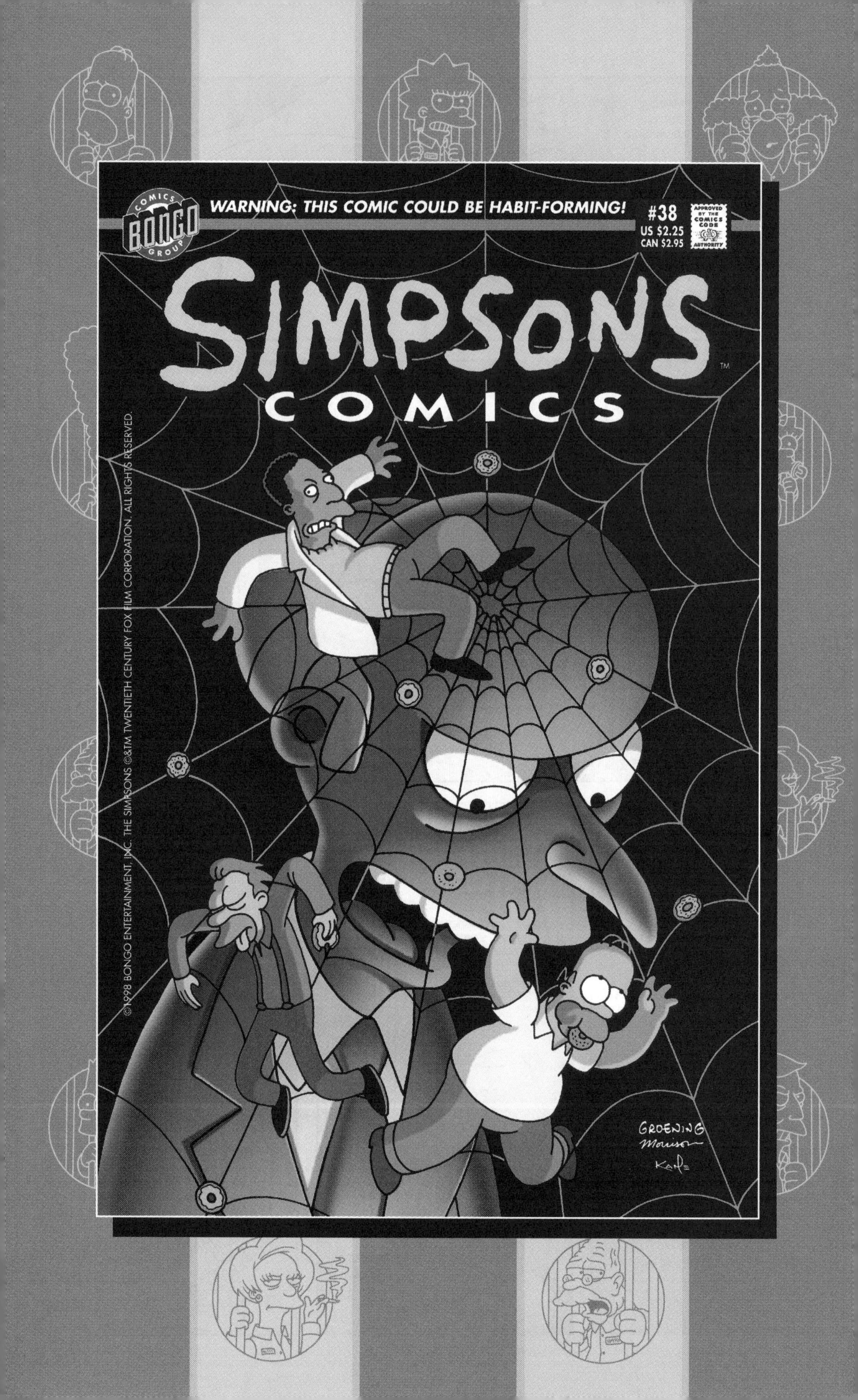
COMICS BONGO GROUP
WARNING: THIS COMIC COULD BE HABIT-FORMING!
#38
US $2.25
CAN $2.95
APPROVED BY THE COMICS CODE AUTHORITY
SIMPSONS™
COMICS
©1998 BONGO ENTERTAINMENT, INC. THE SIMPSONS ©&TM TWENTIETH CENTURY FOX FILM CORPORATION. ALL RIGHTS RESERVED.
GROENING
Morrison
Kane

Smilin' Joe's Sinful Sinkers
better living through deep-fried pastry
DULLARDS TO DONUTS
SCRIPT BILLY RUBENSTEIN
PENCILS PHIL ORTIZ
INKS TIM BAVINGTON
LETTERS JEANNINE BLACK
COLORS NATHAN KANE
LARD LORD MATT GROENING

I'M PARTIAL TO THE SMOOTH, FRUITY TASTE OF THE GRAPE FILLING IN THE JELLY DONUTS. THEY HAVE A PLAYFUL INSOUCIANCE AND A DELECTABLE FLIRTATIOUS AROMA THAT COMPLIMENTS...
REALLY? 'CAUSE I PREFER THE SUPPLE BALANCE OF THE TRADITIONAL POWDERED DONUT. IT'S UNCTUOUS, YET LIVELY.
NO, NO, YOU PLEBEIANS! YOU'VE GOT TO GO WITH THE ROBUST BOUQUET OF THE CRUMB.
THE NOSE, THE COLOR, AND THE BODY OF THE CRUMB DONUT ARE ALL FAR SUPERIOR TO THOSE INELEGANT MORSELS YOU SO PREFER.
HEY HOMER, LET SOMEONE ELSE LICK THE BOX FOR A WHILE.
YEAH, I WANNA TO SEE IF THERE'S ANY JELLY GLOBS LEFT.
SMACK!
MRMPH!
LICK!
CRUMBS, YOU UNSOPHISTICATED BRUTE! THE CRUMB IS THE ONLY DONUT OF THE EDUCATED PALATE!
JELLY!
POWDERED!
CRUMB!
SMACK!
HMMM. THIS DOESN'T SEEM RIGHT.
POWER PLANT EXPENSE REPORT
I ♥ MY BOSS
THE DONUT EXPENSES ARE THROUGH THE ROOF!
pg. 3
POWER PLANT EXPENSE REPORT
Ball Bearings 10,000.00
Hard Hats 500.00
Bongos 25.00
"Contributions"
Unions
Government 100,000.00
Nuclear Regulatory Commission 100,000.00
Environmental Protection Agency 100,000.00
Denture Adhesive (Mr. Burns) 100,000.00
Donuts 1,000.00
200,000.00
Medical Supplies
Sector 7G 50,000.00
Everywhere Else 200.00
I'D BETTER BRING THIS TO MR. BURNS' ATTENTION.
PFENNIGS

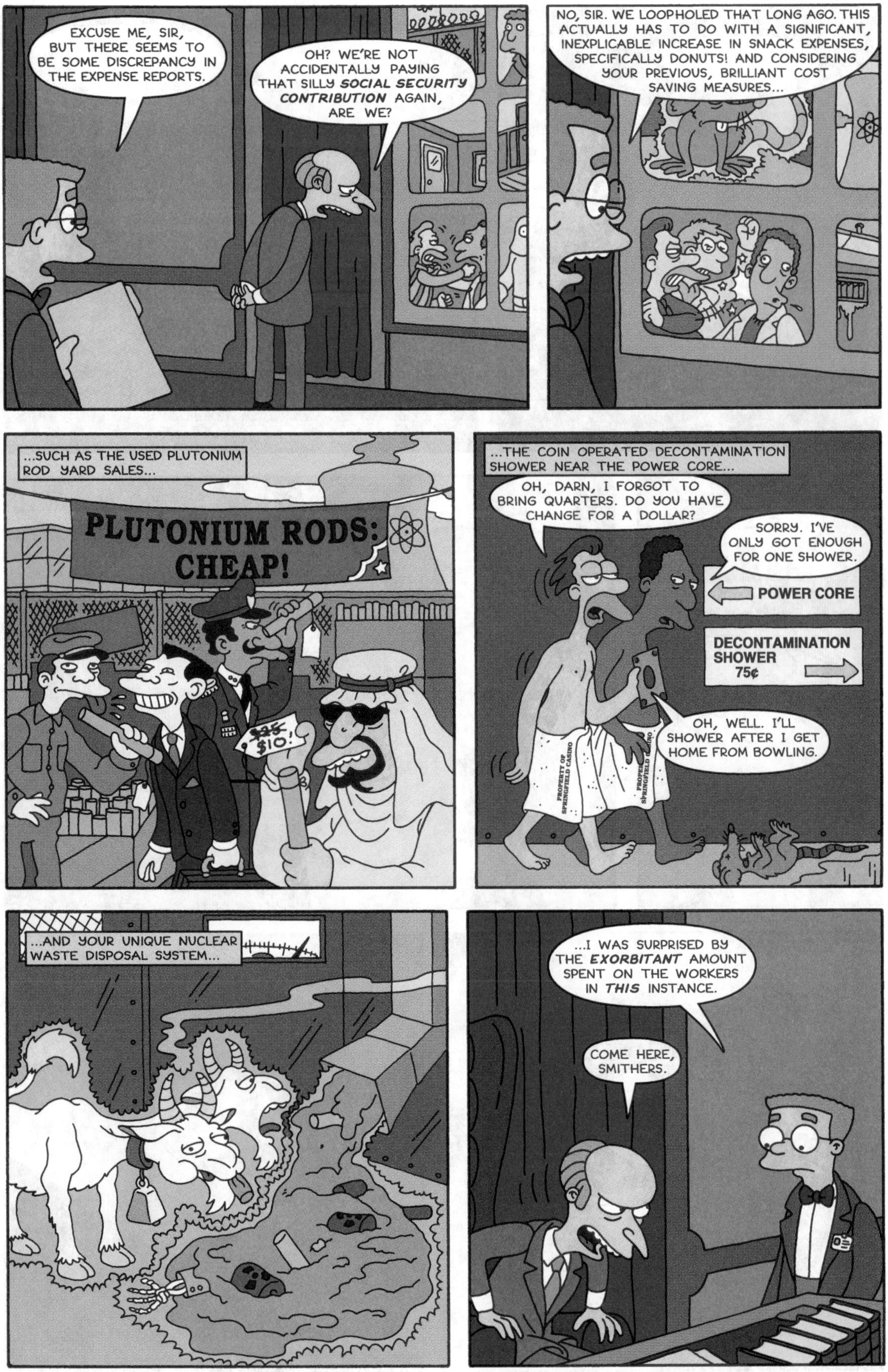

EXCUSE ME, SIR, BUT THERE SEEMS TO BE SOME DISCREPANCY IN THE EXPENSE REPORTS.
OH? WE'RE NOT ACCIDENTALLY PAYING THAT SILLY SOCIAL SECURITY CONTRIBUTION AGAIN, ARE WE?
NO, SIR. WE LOOPHOLED THAT LONG AGO. THIS ACTUALLY HAS TO DO WITH A SIGNIFICANT, INEXPLICABLE INCREASE IN SNACK EXPENSES, SPECIFICALLY DONUTS! AND CONSIDERING YOUR PREVIOUS, BRILLIANT COST SAVING MEASURES...
...SUCH AS THE USED PLUTONIUM ROD YARD SALES...
PLUTONIUM RODS: CHEAP!
$25 $10!
...THE COIN OPERATED DECONTAMINATION SHOWER NEAR THE POWER CORE...
OH, DARN, I FORGOT TO BRING QUARTERS. DO YOU HAVE CHANGE FOR A DOLLAR?
SORRY. I'VE ONLY GOT ENOUGH FOR ONE SHOWER.
POWER CORE
DECONTAMINATION SHOWER 75¢
PROPERTY OF SPRINGFIELD CASINO
OH, WELL. I'LL SHOWER AFTER I GET HOME FROM BOWLING.
...AND YOUR UNIQUE NUCLEAR WASTE DISPOSAL SYSTEM...
...I WAS SURPRISED BY THE EXORBITANT AMOUNT SPENT ON THE WORKERS IN THIS INSTANCE.
COME HERE, SMITHERS.

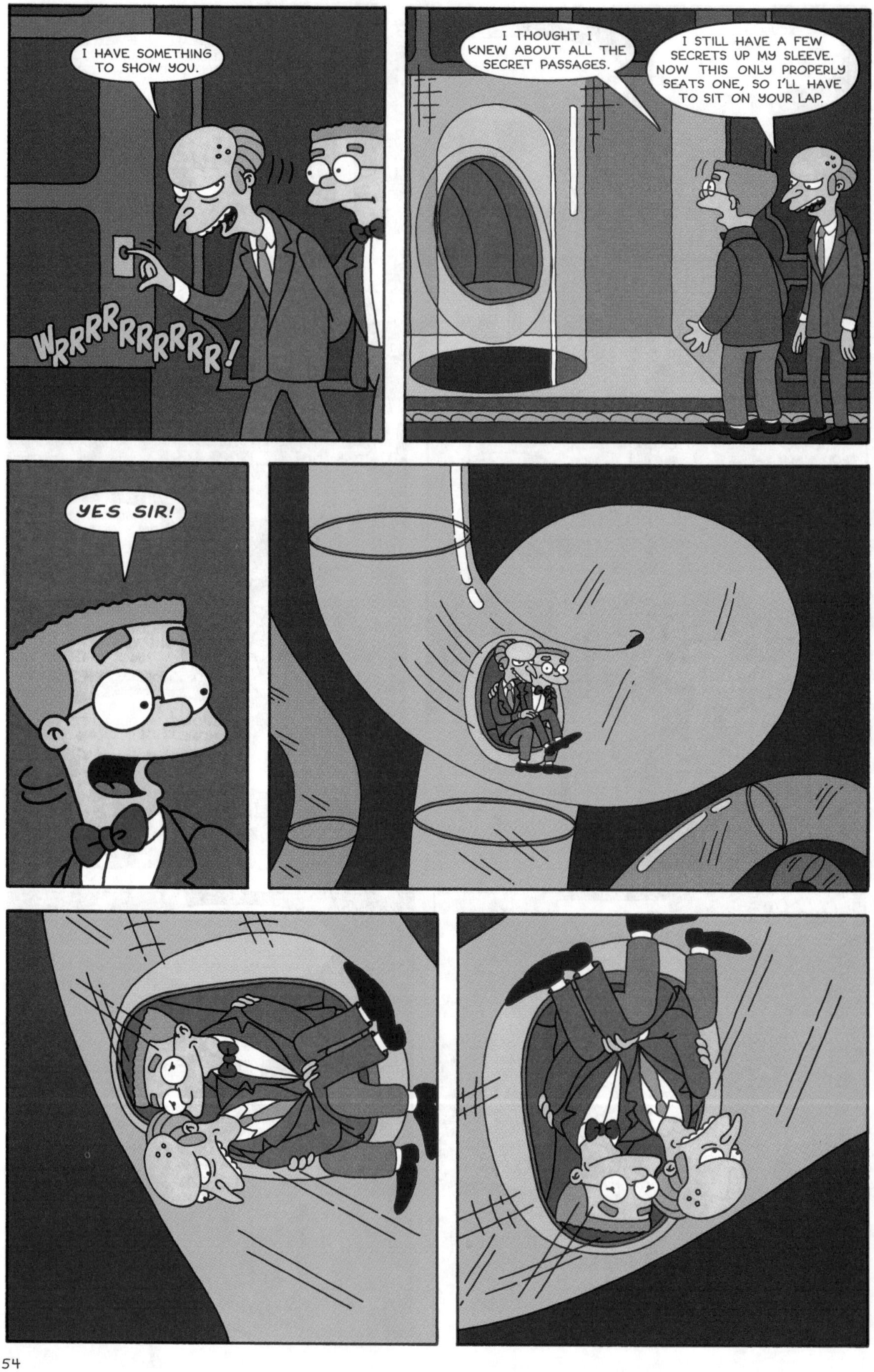
I HAVE SOMETHING TO SHOW YOU.
WRRRRRRRRRRR!
I THOUGHT I KNEW ABOUT ALL THE SECRET PASSAGES.
I STILL HAVE A FEW SECRETS UP MY SLEEVE. NOW THIS ONLY PROPERLY SEATS ONE, SO I'LL HAVE TO SIT ON YOUR LAP.
YES SIR!

VOOP!
SMITHERS, I BELIEVE YOU KNOW THE ESTEEMED SCIENTIST, DR. OLBERMAN.
OF COURSE, SIR.
SO WHAT ARE YOU WORKING ON?
THAT!
HEY!
FWAP!
OBSERVE.
LARD LAD DONUTS

NOTE HOW THE MONKEYS COULD NOT CARE LESS FOR YOUR AVERAGE PASTRY.
POKE POKE
SPRINGFIELD TIMES
NOW WATCH THIS.
THEY SEE THE DONUT.
THWIP!
...AND THEY MUST HAVE IT!
BIFF!
POW!
ZONK!
SLUG!
AMAZING! IT'S LIKE THE MONKEYS NEED THOSE DONUTS.
DEVELOPING THESE HIGHLY DESIRABLE DONUTS WAS THE EASY PART. CREATING A MARKETING CAMPAIGN THAT WOULD APPEAL TO BOTH CURRENT AND FUTURE USERS, NOW THAT WAS A CHALLENGE.
OH, YES, THEY CANNOT HELP THEMSELVES.
BUT I BELIEVE WE SUCCEEDED ON BOTH FRONTS BY USING A CARTOON CHARACTER, SINCE PEOPLE ARE SUCKERS FOR ANYTHING THAT IS ENDORSED BY A FICTIONAL, ANIMATED FIGURE.
Trade in coupons on boxes for cool stuff!
SMILIN' JOE
EXCELLENT!

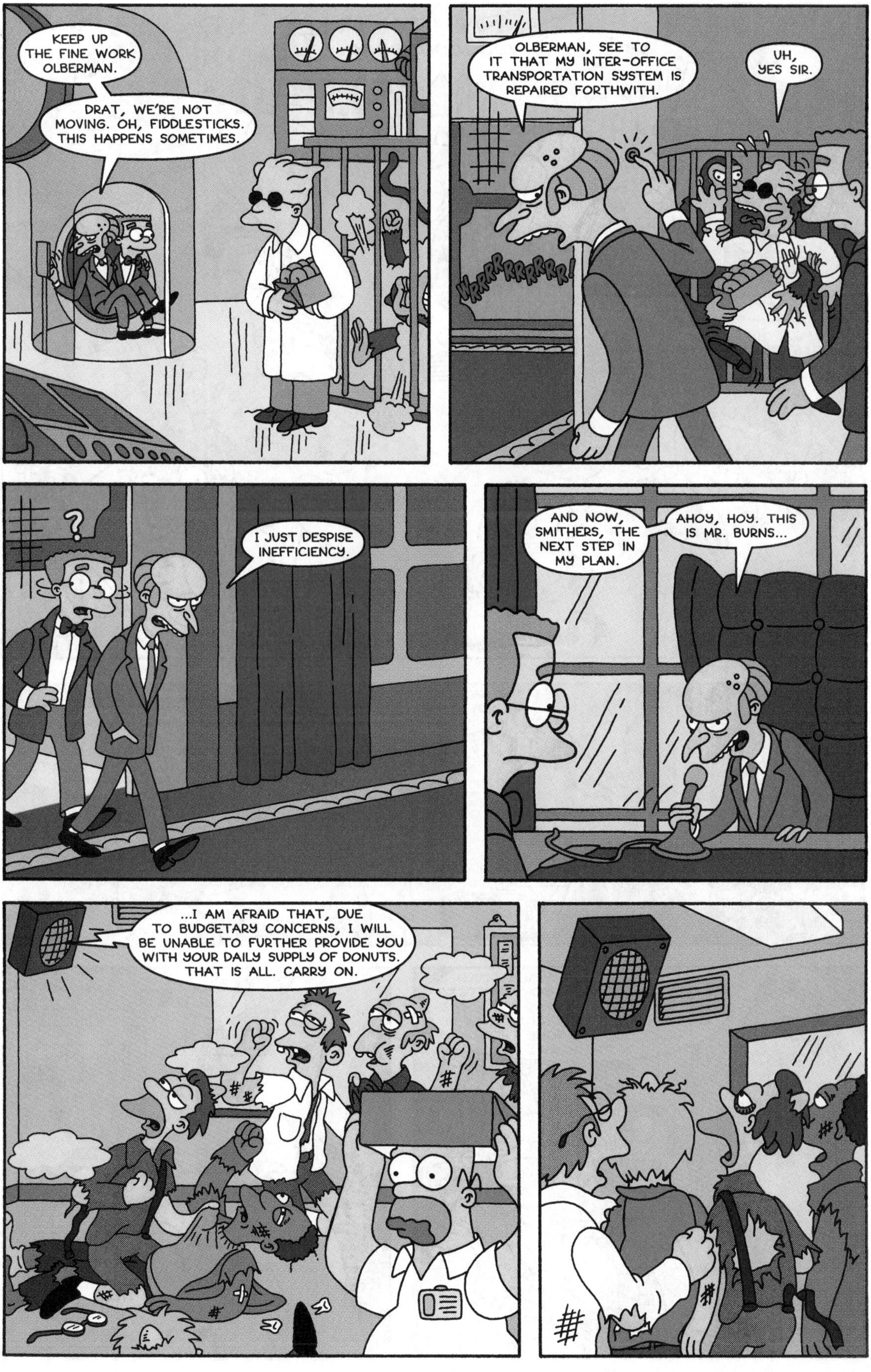
KEEP UP THE FINE WORK OLBERMAN.
DRAT, WE'RE NOT MOVING. OH, FIDDLESTICKS. THIS HAPPENS SOMETIMES.
OLBERMAN, SEE TO IT THAT MY INTER-OFFICE TRANSPORTATION SYSTEM IS REPAIRED FORTHWITH.
UH, YES SIR.
WRRRRRRRRRR!
I JUST DESPISE INEFFICIENCY.
AND NOW, SMITHERS, THE NEXT STEP IN MY PLAN.
AHOY, HOY. THIS IS MR. BURNS...
...I AM AFRAID THAT, DUE TO BUDGETARY CONCERNS, I WILL BE UNABLE TO FURTHER PROVIDE YOU WITH YOUR DAILY SUPPLY OF DONUTS. THAT IS ALL. CARRY ON.

NOOOOOOOOOOOO!
NOT THE DONUTS! TAKE MY *FAMILY*, BUT NOT *THE DONUTS!*
LATER...
HOMEY, WHAT ARE YOU *DOING*? IT'S FOUR IN THE MORNING.
DONUTS? WHERE ARE THE DONUTS?! FOR THE LOVE OF GOD, MARGE, *PLEASE* TELL ME YOU'VE GOT *DONUTS* HERE SOMEWHERE!
HOMER CALM DOWN. YOU STOPPED EATING STORE-BOUGHT DONUTS *WEEKS* AGO, SO I STOPPED BUYING THEM. *THE KWIK-E-MART* HAS DONUTS, SO WHY DON'T YOU GET SOME THERE IN THE MORN...
...ING
SLAM!

BABY, BABY, BABY. WHERE DID OUR LOVE GO? DON'T YOU WANT ME? DON'T YOU WANT ME NO MORE?
BABY! BABY! AND IT IS HURTING ME SO BAD!
KIRK 'N' KRUSTY KOVER THE KLASSICS
KWIK E MART
OH GOODNESS GRACIOUS ME!
THEY'VE EATEN EVERY DONUT IN STOCK. EVEN THE KRUSTOFSKI'S KOSHER UNLEAVENED DONUTS!
HOLY MATZO!
OHH. THESE DONUTS DON'T MAKE ME FEEL GOOD LIKE THE ONES AT THE PLANT.
YEAH, ME NEITHER.
BESIDES, THIS IS HUMILIATING. I'VE GOT SOME DIGNITY YOU KNOW.
PLEASE! PLEASE! PLEASE!
I STILL THINK NOT. I'M AFRAID THERE'S NO MORE MONEY FOR SNACKS.
WE ALL HAVE TO MAKE CONCESSIONS DURING TIMES OF FINANCIAL HARDSHIP.
BESIDES, THAT WAS A NAMBY-PAMBY PONY RIDE.
D'OH!
NUTS!
DONUTS, YOU SAY? YOU REALLY WANT THE DONUTS THAT BADLY, EH? PERHAPS WE COULD WORK OUT SOME SORT OF QUID PRO QUO. SAY, HALF YOUR PAY AND BENEFITS IN EXCHANGE FOR YOUR PRECIOUS DONUTS?
YES!
WOO-HOO!
SMEK!
AND WE STILL HAVE OUR DIGNITY!

THAT NIGHT...
...AND SO... ⸗MRMF⸗...FAMILY, THERE'S GOING TO BE...⸗HARPH⸗...SOME CUTBACKS AROUND HERE...⸗MUNCH⸗...
HOMER, HOW CAN WE GET BY ON HALF YOUR PAY?
I'VE GOT IT ALL FIGURED OUT. YOU WON'T HAVE TO BUY FOOD FOR ME BECAUSE MR. BURNS IS GIVING US ALL THE DONUTS WE WANT.
HOMER! YOU CAN'T LIVE ON DONUTS ALONE!
OF COURSE NOT, MARGE. I'LL NEED COFFEE FOR DUNKING AND WASHING THEM DOWN.
OH, AND BEER.
BOY! DON'T EVER TRY TO TAKE ONE OF THESE DONUTS!
EASY THERE HOME-BOY. I JUST WANT THE COUPON ON THE BOX TO TRADE IN FOR T-SHIRTS AND STUFF.
HOMER, I DON'T KNOW WHAT'S GOTTEN INTO YOU LATELY, BUT I DON'T WANT YOU TAKING YOUR PROBLEMS OUT ON THE KIDS.
YOINK!
THAT'S IT! YOU DON'T UNDERSTAND ME! I NEED TO BE ALONE FOR AWHILE, BY MYSELF, WHERE NO ONE CAN FIND ME. I'M GOING TO MOE'S!
HOMER, AREN'T YOU FORGETTING SOMETHING?
OH, YEAH.
THANKS, MARGE.

THE NEXT DAY...
WHERE IS IT THAT WE WOULD FIND THE SHOVELS, THE RUBBER GLOVES, THE PLASTIC TARPS, AND THE STUBBORN STAIN REMOVERS?
Sale
Get a free carton of "dairy-free lactose" with each box. Now with more lactose!
AISLE THREE, NEXT TO THE POWDERED LIME.
JERKY LOGS
WOULD YOU CARE TO LET ME INTEREST YOU IN A BOX OF DONUTS TODAY? THEY ARE PRICED TO MOVE.
NO THANK YOU, APU. HOMER ONLY EATS THE DONUTS HE GETS AT THE POWER PLANT.
YES, YES. I HAVE NOTICED THIS AS WELL. MY SUPPLY OF DONUTS HAS SOLD NOT AT ALL. I WOULD SELL THOSE DONUTS AT A CONSIDERABLE MARK-UP, BUT I AM WITHOUT AN IDEA AS TO HOW TO OBTAIN THEM.
I KNOW. I CAN'T FIND THEM ANYWHERE EITHER. I WANT TO KNOW WHAT'S IN THEM. IT'S LIKE THEY'RE HABIT-FORMING OR SOMETHING.
GENTLEMEN, IT APPEARS THAT THERE IS A CONTROLLED SUBSTANCE IN THIS TOWN THAT IS NOT WITHIN OUR CONTROL. THIS DISTURBS ME GREATLY. WE MUST GO NOW.
BUT WHAT ABOUT THIS STUFF FOR THE YOU KNOW WHAT?
OH, YES, THAT. LOUIE, IT IS YOUR LUCKY DAY. YOU GET TO LIVE.
ALL RIGHT! I MEAN, HEY, WAIT A SECOND!
EVER SINCE THOSE DONUTS HAVE APPEARED, MY BUSINESS HAS BEEN DOWN QUITE A PRETTY PENNY.
HEY MOM, CAN I HAVE A BANGLADESHI SQUISHEE? CAN I? HUH? CAN I?
AND MAY I HAVE SOME ORGANIC GOOEY CHEWY BEARS? MAY I? PLEASE? MAY I?
NO TO BOTH OF YOU. YOU KNOW WE ALL HAVE TO CUT BACK ON EXTRAVAGANT SPENDING SINCE YOUR FATHER TOOK THAT PAY CUT.
AWWWW.
YOU SEE? THIS IS THAT ABOUT WHICH I HAVE BEEN SAYING. IF THIS KEEPS UP... ...I AM ACTUALLY GOING TO HAVE TO OFFER COMPETITIVE PRICES, AND THEN IT'S NO "ZEN AND THE ART OF THE MONSTER TRUCK PULL FANTASY CAMP" FOR ME.
HMMM. I WONDER IF ANYONE ELSE HAS BEEN AFFECTED?

I DON'T WANT TO BE A GRIPERINSKI, BUT BUSINESS AT THE LEFTORIUM **HAS** BEEN DOWN MIGHTILY-ITILY AS OF LATE. I PROMISED ROD AND TODD I'D TAKE THEM TO SEE THE "RELIGIOUS OVERTONES JAZZ BAND", BUT I DON'T KNOW IF I'LL BE ABLE TO **AFFORD** IT.
HMMM.
LEFT HANDERS RULE!
I ♥ SOUTH PAWS
POSTERS

AND BECAUSE THE PRIMARY WAGE PROVIDERS OF THIS COMMUNITY NO LONGER BESTOW THEIR LARGESS ON THEIR LITTLE RUGRATS, I HAVE AN UNWANTED SURPLUS OF RADIOACTIVE MAN AND SUPERIOR SQUAD PARAPHERNALIA. BECAUSE OF MY FINANCIAL STRAITS, I WILL NOT BE ABLE TO ATTEND THIS YEAR'S TRIBUTE TO THE UNDER APPRECIATED SCI-FI WORK OF THE GREAT RICARDO MONTALBAN AT THE "CANNES KHAN CON."
HMMM.

YES, MARGE, OUR COFFERS ARE RUNNING QUITE DRY AT THE MOMENT. I WAS HOPING TO ADD A STROBE LIGHT AND DOLBY SOUND SYSTEM TO OUR NATIVITY SCENE THIS YEAR, BUT AT THIS RATE, WE'LL BE LUCKY IF WE CAN AFFORD **TWO** WISE MEN.
HMMM.
Raspberry Sparkling Holy Water
Where's Waldo In The Bible
MODEL TRAINS MONTHLY

YOU WANT A SPECIAL TOWN HALL MEETING TO...AH... DETERMINE IF THE DONUTS AT THE POWER PLANT POSE...AHEM...A SERIOUS HEALTH THREAT? YOU **GOT** IT. SALES AND INCOME TAXES ARE SO FAR DOWN, I'VE HAD TO CANCEL THREE...EH...JUNKETS AND FOUR TRYSTS. I DON'T CARE HOW MUCH BURNS IS BRIBING ME...AHEM...I MEAN HOW MUCH MONEY MR. BURNS HAS, THE FINANCES OF SPRINGFIELD'S PROSTITU...ER...I MEAN POPULACE, COMES FIRST!
MAYOR QUIMBY

MEANWHILE...
SMITHERS, WHAT'S THE MEANING OF THIS? WHY ARE THERE PEOPLE PROTESTING OUTSIDE MY PLANT?
NUCLEAR POWER IS DA BOMB!
SMILIN' JOE, YOU'RE SO SEXY!
Get that Sinful, Sinkin' Feeling!
Sinful Sinkers: The Real Devil's Food Cake
What's the deal with the hole?
STOP TARGETING OUR KIDS
What's in those things anyway?
GABBO RULES!

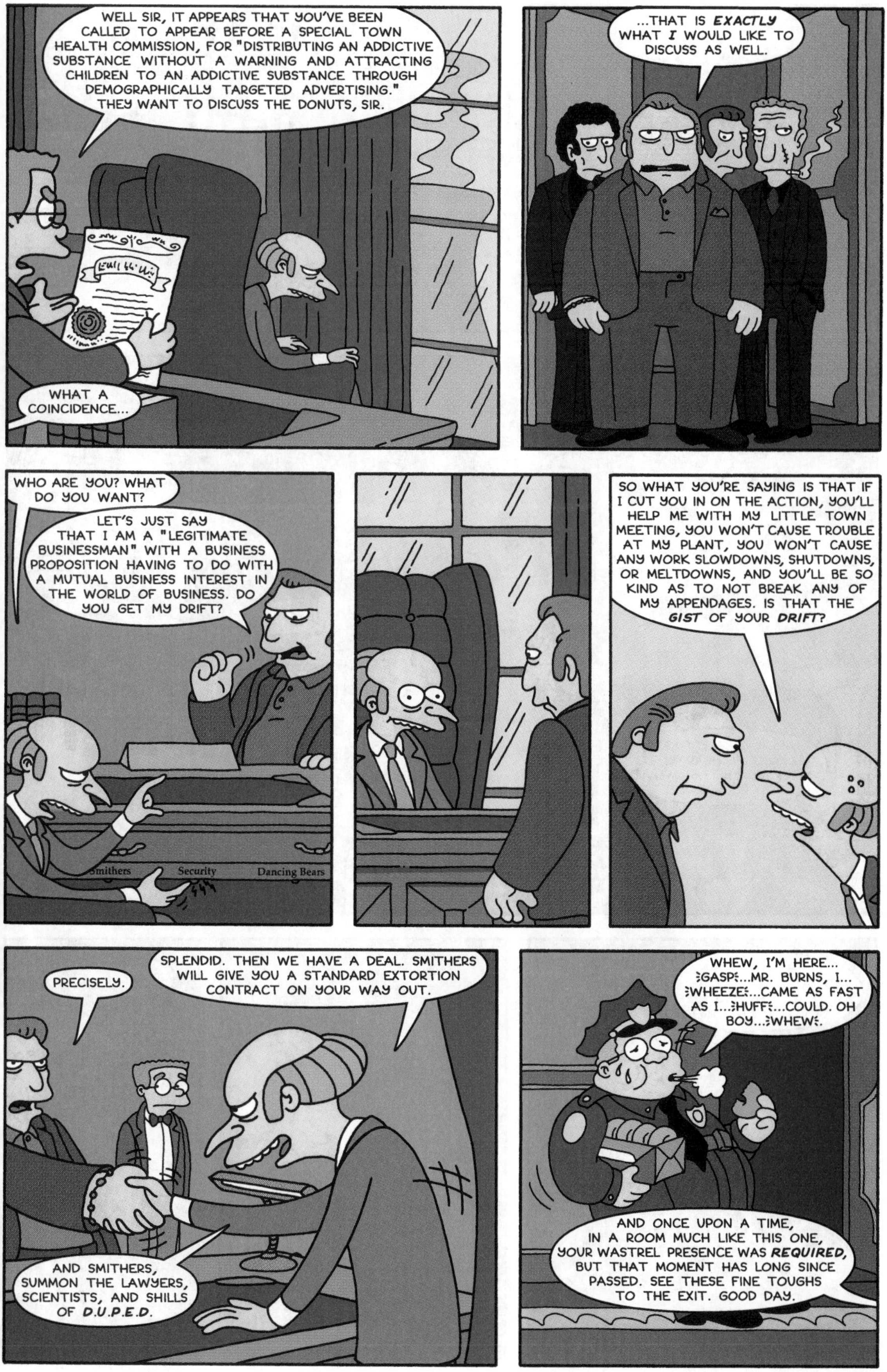
WELL SIR, IT APPEARS THAT YOU'VE BEEN CALLED TO APPEAR BEFORE A SPECIAL TOWN HEALTH COMMISSION, FOR "DISTRIBUTING AN ADDICTIVE SUBSTANCE WITHOUT A WARNING AND ATTRACTING CHILDREN TO AN ADDICTIVE SUBSTANCE THROUGH DEMOGRAPHICALLY TARGETED ADVERTISING." THEY WANT TO DISCUSS THE DONUTS, SIR.
WHAT A COINCIDENCE...
...THAT IS EXACTLY WHAT I WOULD LIKE TO DISCUSS AS WELL.
WHO ARE YOU? WHAT DO YOU WANT?
LET'S JUST SAY THAT I AM A "LEGITIMATE BUSINESSMAN" WITH A BUSINESS PROPOSITION HAVING TO DO WITH A MUTUAL BUSINESS INTEREST IN THE WORLD OF BUSINESS. DO YOU GET MY DRIFT?
Smithers
Security
Dancing Bears
SO WHAT YOU'RE SAYING IS THAT IF I CUT YOU IN ON THE ACTION, YOU'LL HELP ME WITH MY LITTLE TOWN MEETING, YOU WON'T CAUSE TROUBLE AT MY PLANT, YOU WON'T CAUSE ANY WORK SLOWDOWNS, SHUTDOWNS, OR MELTDOWNS, AND YOU'LL BE SO KIND AS TO NOT BREAK ANY OF MY APPENDAGES. IS THAT THE GIST OF YOUR DRIFT?
PRECISELY.
SPLENDID. THEN WE HAVE A DEAL. SMITHERS WILL GIVE YOU A STANDARD EXTORTION CONTRACT ON YOUR WAY OUT.
AND SMITHERS, SUMMON THE LAWYERS, SCIENTISTS, AND SHILLS OF D.U.P.E.D.
WHEW, I'M HERE... ;GASP;...MR. BURNS, I... ;WHEEZE;...CAME AS FAST AS I...;HUFF;...COULD. OH BOY...;WHEW;.
AND ONCE UPON A TIME, IN A ROOM MUCH LIKE THIS ONE, YOUR WASTREL PRESENCE WAS REQUIRED, BUT THAT MOMENT HAS LONG SINCE PASSED. SEE THESE FINE TOUGHS TO THE EXIT. GOOD DAY.

I'M KENT BROCKMAN FOR "SMARTLINE". TONIGHT, SMILIN' JOE'S SINFUL SINKERS. A TASTY PASTRY THAT'S NUTRITIOUS AND GOOD FOR THE WHOLE FAMILY, OR A PRODUCT WRONGFULLY ACCUSED BY A BUNCH OF OVERZEALOUS SAFETY FREAKS WITH TOO MUCH TIME ON THEIR HANDS?
CITY HALL
TONIGHT: SPECIAL HEALTH COMMISSION EXAMINES DONUTS.
TOMORROW: SPECIAL VIDEO COMMISSION EXAMINES PORN (BYO PORN & DONUTS).
WE'LL BE BACK WITH THIS REPORT RIGHT AFTER THIS MESSAGE FROM OUR NEW SPONSOR, SMILIN' JOE'S SINFUL SINKERS.
6

AHEM. I CALL THIS... EH...SPECIAL HEARING TO ORDER. MR. BURNS, WOULD YOU PLEASE RISE?

DO YOU...EH...SWEAR TO TELL THE TRUTH, THE WHOLE TRUTH, AND NOTHING BUT THE...EH...TRUTH?

I DO.

I AM JUST AN OLD, SIMPLE MAN. I KNOW VERY LITTLE ABOUT GORMANDIZING HABITS, NUTRITIONAL SCIENCE, OR ANY OF THESE OTHER COMPLICATED MATTERS. I MERELY WANT TO GIVE MY WELL-DESERVING WORKERS A LITTLE EXTRA SOMETHING BACK IN EXCHANGE FOR ALL OF THEIR SWEAT AND TOIL.
THEY SEEM TO LIKE THESE ROUND, PASTRY TREATS WITH THE WHIMSICAL HOLE IN THE MIDDLE, SO THAT'S WHAT I GIVE THEM.
MMM...WHIMSICAL HOLE.
NOW AS FOR THE SCIENCE OF THE MATTER, I GIVE YOU MY ESTEEMED COLLEAGUE, ***DR. OLBERMAN,*** FROM THE ***D***ONUT ***U***NION ***P***UBLIC ***E***DUCATION ***D***IVISION.
I KNOW HOW DRY AND INTIMIDATING COMPLICATED SCIENTIFIC MATTERS CAN BE TO THE LAYPERSON, SO I'M GOING TO TRY AND KEEP IT SIMPLE.
MEMORY
HAPPINESS
HUNGER
WOO-HOO!
ALL RIGHT!
SIMPLIFY!
MEMORY
HAPPINESS
HUNGER
DONUTS ARE NOT ONLY ***NOT*** HARMFUL, THEY ACTUALLY PROVIDE MANY NEUROLOGICAL BENEFITS, SUCH AS REDUCING STRESS, IMPROVING MEMORY, AND DECREASING APPETITES. IN FACT, EVERY TEST WE'VE CONDUCTED CONCLUSIVELY PROVES THAT AFTER CONSUMING DONUTS, THE SUBJECTS ARE LESS HUNGRY, THEY ARE HAPPIER, AND THEY CAN REMEMBER ***WHY*** THEY ARE HAPPY.
AS YOU CAN IN SEE IN CHART TWO, THE UNIQUE CONFIGURATION IN THE MOLECULAR STRUCTURE THAT IS THE BASIS OF THE DONUT WORKS IN A COMPLIMENTARY FASHION WITH THE EPITHELIAL CELLS FROM THE STOMACH LINING...
...AND CHART SEVENTY-SIX CLEARLY DEMONSTRATES HOW EACH DONUT HAS A UNIQUE DNA BLUEPRINT WHICH PROVIDES THE YUMMY FLAVOR THAT YOU ENJOY SO MUCH. SO, IN CONCLUSION, AS A MEMBER OF THE NON-BIASED, IMPARTIAL SCIENTIFIC COMMUNITY, I BELIEVE THAT NOT ONLY ARE THESE DONUTS NOT HARMFUL, THEY ARE ACTUALLY QUITE BENEFICIAL TO THOSE WHO CONSUME THEM. THANK YOU.
EVERYBODY WAKE UP! HE'S FINISHED!

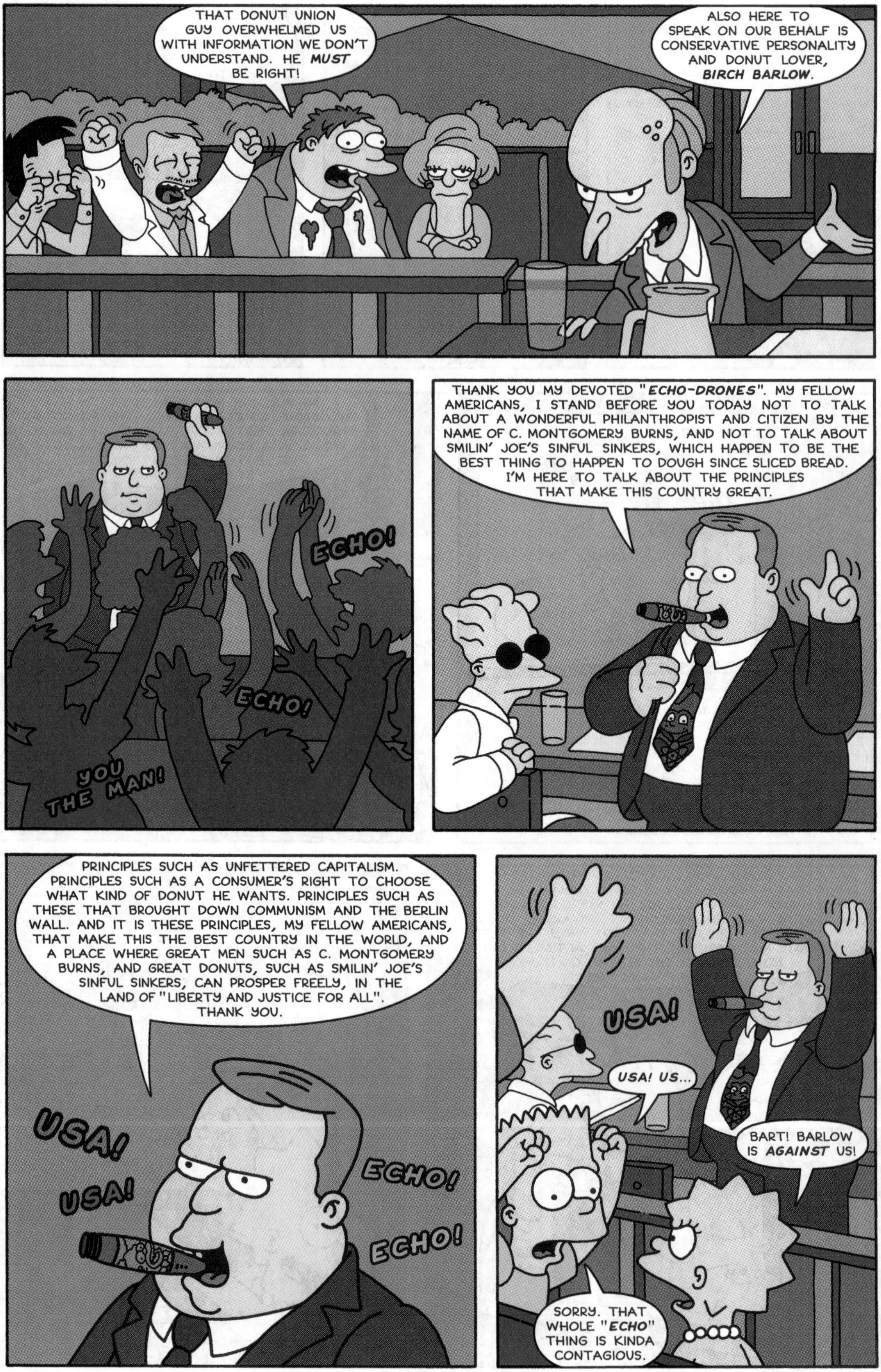
THAT DONUT UNION GUY OVERWHELMED US WITH INFORMATION WE DON'T UNDERSTAND. HE MUST BE RIGHT!
ALSO HERE TO SPEAK ON OUR BEHALF IS CONSERVATIVE PERSONALITY AND DONUT LOVER, BIRCH BARLOW.
ECHO!
ECHO!
YOU THE MAN!
THANK YOU MY DEVOTED "ECHO-DRONES". MY FELLOW AMERICANS, I STAND BEFORE YOU TODAY NOT TO TALK ABOUT A WONDERFUL PHILANTHROPIST AND CITIZEN BY THE NAME OF C. MONTGOMERY BURNS, AND NOT TO TALK ABOUT SMILIN' JOE'S SINFUL SINKERS, WHICH HAPPEN TO BE THE BEST THING TO HAPPEN TO DOUGH SINCE SLICED BREAD. I'M HERE TO TALK ABOUT THE PRINCIPLES THAT MAKE THIS COUNTRY GREAT.
PRINCIPLES SUCH AS UNFETTERED CAPITALISM. PRINCIPLES SUCH AS A CONSUMER'S RIGHT TO CHOOSE WHAT KIND OF DONUT HE WANTS. PRINCIPLES SUCH AS THESE THAT BROUGHT DOWN COMMUNISM AND THE BERLIN WALL. AND IT IS THESE PRINCIPLES, MY FELLOW AMERICANS, THAT MAKE THIS THE BEST COUNTRY IN THE WORLD, AND A PLACE WHERE GREAT MEN SUCH AS C. MONTGOMERY BURNS, AND GREAT DONUTS, SUCH AS SMILIN' JOE'S SINFUL SINKERS, CAN PROSPER FREELY, IN THE LAND OF "LIBERTY AND JUSTICE FOR ALL". THANK YOU.
USA!
USA!
ECHO!
ECHO!
USA!
USA! US...
BART! BARLOW IS AGAINST US!
SORRY. THAT WHOLE "ECHO" THING IS KINDA CONTAGIOUS.

I...EH...WOULD LIKE TO THANK **BIRCH BARLOW** FOR HIS...AHEM... REMARKS AND WOULD LIKE TO REMIND ALL OF HIS LOYAL FANS WHO VOTE FOR WHOEVER HE TELLS THEM TO THAT I...AHEM... CONSIDER ***MYSELF*** AN "***ECHO-DRONE***". NOW, IS THERE...EH... ANYONE ELSE WHO WOULD LIKE TO SPEAK?
I HAVE SOMETHING I'D LIKE TO SAY.
THE CHAIR RECOGNIZES THE WOMAN WITH THE...EH... UNIQUE HAIRDO.
MY NAME IS MARGE SIMPSON, AND I DON'T HAVE ANY SCIENTISTS OR FAMOUS PERSONALITIES TO BACK ME UP...
...BUT I KNOW THAT AS A WIFE, A MOTHER, AND A CONCERNED MEMBER OF THIS COMMUNITY THAT I'M WORRIED ABOUT THE EFFECTS THAT THESE DONUTS ARE HAVING.
THEY HAVE NO NUTRITIONAL VALUE, THEY'RE BANKRUPTING EVERYONE EXCEPT MR. BURNS, THE ADVERTISEMENTS ARE AIMED AT CHILDREN, AND ALTHOUGH I CAN'T PROVE IT, I'D SWEAR THAT THEY'RE *ADDICTIVE*.
SHE HAS A POINT.
I HADN'T THOUGHT OF THAT.
THAT'S TRUE.
I'M THE OWNER OF ***LARD LAD DONUTS,*** AND NO ONE IS TAKING ***MY*** BUSINESS WITHOUT A ***FIGHT!*** I HAD ONE OF THESE SMILIN' JOE'S SINFUL SINKERS EXAMINED...
...AND WHAT I FOUND IN THEM WAS ***SHOCKING!*** WHAT I FOUND WAS...
NOW!
WHAT'S GOING ON?!
PARDON ME.
COMING THROUGH!
BAM!

WELL MY DEAR LADY, IT SEEMED RATHER INAPPROPRIATE TO HAVE AN ENTIRE DISCUSSION ABOUT MY DONUTS WITHOUT HAVING THEM IN THE ROOM. DOESN'T THAT MAKE SENSE?
WELL, I GUESS, BUT, UM, I'M NOT SURE, WELL, NO, BUT...
THESE ARE THE BEST DONUTS I'VE EVER TASTED! AND *I* KNOW DONUTS!
THEY HAVE NO NUTRITIONAL VALUE, THEY'RE LOADED WITH FAT, AND ARE PROBABLY CLOGGING MY ARTERIES AS WE SPEAK, BUT MY, ARE THEY DELICIOUS. HEH, HEH, HEH!
CAN I GET THESE FOR THE SCHOOL?
I HEREBY...:MUNCH:... CALL TO CLOSE THIS...:MRPH:... MEETING, SO THAT WE CAN ALL GET SOME MORE DONUTS, SOME MILK AND SOME...:AHEM:... COFFEE, OR WHATEVER BEVERAGE MR. BARLOW TELLS US WE WANT.
AREN'T YOU AT LEAST GOING TO DO ANYTHING TO WARN PEOPLE ABOUT THE ***HEALTH RISKS*** OF TOO MANY DONUTS?
YOUNG LADY, YOU HAVE A VALID POINT, AND... AHEM...LET ME ***ASSURE*** YOU THAT YOUR CONCERNS WILL BE TAKEN ***SERIOUSLY***.
WARNING!
It is believed by some that consuming these donuts in great quantities constitutes a health risk. We think those people are morons. You're not a moron, are you?
I WANT TO BE LIKE ***SMILIN' JOE!***
NOW: Smilin' Joe's Sinful Sinkers are available at the Springfield Elementary school cafeteria!
SPRINGFIELD ELEMENTARY
COOL!
CHECK HIM OUT!
Better living through deep-fried pastry

WEEKS LATER...
HMMM. THIS DOESN'T LOOK GOOD.
I ♥ MY BOSS
EXPENDITURES ON DONUTS
WORKER PRODUCTIVITY
SMITHERS, WHAT IS THE MEANING OF THIS? I'M GIVING THESE WORKERS ALL THE DONUTS THEY WANT. WHY ARE THEY NOW LESS EFFICIENT?
SIR, I THINK THE ANSWER IS ON THE MONITORS.
DANGER!
WARNING

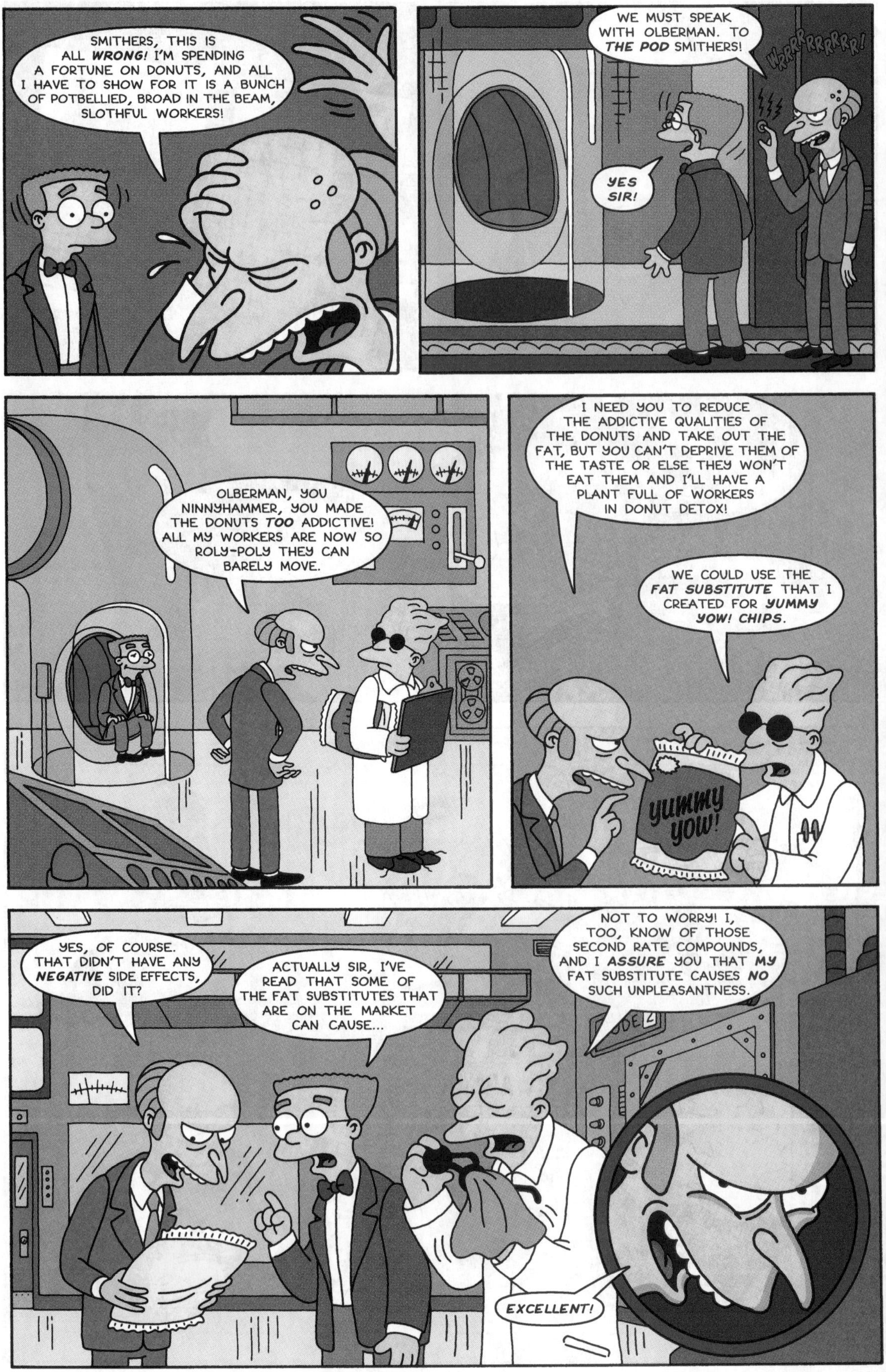
SMITHERS, THIS IS ALL **WRONG!** I'M SPENDING A FORTUNE ON DONUTS, AND ALL I HAVE TO SHOW FOR IT IS A BUNCH OF POTBELLIED, BROAD IN THE BEAM, SLOTHFUL WORKERS!
WE MUST SPEAK WITH OLBERMAN. TO **THE POD** SMITHERS!
WRRRRRRRRRRR!
YES SIR!
OLBERMAN, YOU NINNYHAMMER, YOU MADE THE DONUTS **TOO** ADDICTIVE! ALL MY WORKERS ARE NOW SO ROLY-POLY THEY CAN BARELY MOVE.
I NEED YOU TO REDUCE THE ADDICTIVE QUALITIES OF THE DONUTS AND TAKE OUT THE FAT, BUT YOU CAN'T DEPRIVE THEM OF THE TASTE OR ELSE THEY WON'T EAT THEM AND I'LL HAVE A PLANT FULL OF WORKERS IN DONUT DETOX!
WE COULD USE THE **FAT SUBSTITUTE** THAT I CREATED FOR **YUMMY YOW! CHIPS**.
YUMMY YOW!
YES, OF COURSE. THAT DIDN'T HAVE ANY **NEGATIVE** SIDE EFFECTS, DID IT?
ACTUALLY SIR, I'VE READ THAT SOME OF THE FAT SUBSTITUTES THAT ARE ON THE MARKET CAN CAUSE...
NOT TO WORRY! I, TOO, KNOW OF THOSE SECOND RATE COMPOUNDS, AND I **ASSURE** YOU THAT **MY** FAT SUBSTITUTE CAUSES **NO** SUCH UNPLEASANTNESS.
EXCELLENT!

St. Frankie De Frugal's 4th Hand Store
BIG BEN'S SECOND HAND STORE
THE TROUBLED CHILD'S 3RD HAND STORE
WHACKERS - 50% OFF!
SALE
BOB WOODWARD'S THE TRUTH ABOUT WHACKING DAY BOOK
WAAAAAH! I MISS MY DONUTS!
IT'S BEEN TWO MONTHS. WHEN DO YOU THINK HE'S GONNA GET OVER THIS?
I DUNNO. I HAVEN'T SEEN HIM THIS BAD SINCE DUFF STOPPED MAKING COFFEE BEER.
MOM, I'M SO PROUD OF YOU. YOU SAW A PROBLEM IN SOCIETY, AND INSTEAD OF SITTING ON THE SIDELINES, YOU DID SOMETHING ABOUT IT. EVEN THOUGH, TECHNICALLY, YOUR INVOLVEMENT HAD NOTHING TO DO WITH THE RESOLUTION, AND THE PROBLEM EVENTUALLY TOOK CARE OF ITSELF.
SQUISHEE
YEAH, AND NOW THAT DAD'S GOT HIS SALARY BACK, WE DON'T HAVE TO SUFFER WITHOUT LIFE'S NECESSITIES. THANKS FOR NOTHING MOM!
YOU SEE KIDS, WHEN YOU PUT YOUR MIND TO IT, YOU CAN ACCOMPLISH ANYTHING-- EVEN ACCIDENTALLY. ALTHOUGH I'M NOT TOO PLEASED WITH THE SIDE EFFECTS OF THESE NEW DONUTS.
GANGWAY! CLEAR A PATH TO THE BATHROOM! BAD CASE COMING THROUGH!
BUT I THOUGHT THESE NEW FAT SUBSTITUTES WEREN'T SUPPOSED TO CAUSE...
OH, THEY DON'T CAUSE THAT. THEY JUST GIVE YOUR FATHER A BAD CASE OF HALITOSIS.
EWW, WHAT'S THAT?
AHHHH! THAT'S MUCH BETTER.
IN LAYMAN'S TERMS, BART, IT'S A BAD CASE OF BAD BREATH. SO I MAKE YOUR FATHER BRUSH HIS TEETH BEFORE I'LL LET HIM GET CLOSE TO ME.
OH. WELL I GUESS THAT'S MUCH BETTER THAN...
IT CERTAINLY IS, BART. IT MOST CERTAINLY IS.
HOMEY, COULD YOU TURN YOUR MOUTH THE OTHER WAY?
THE END

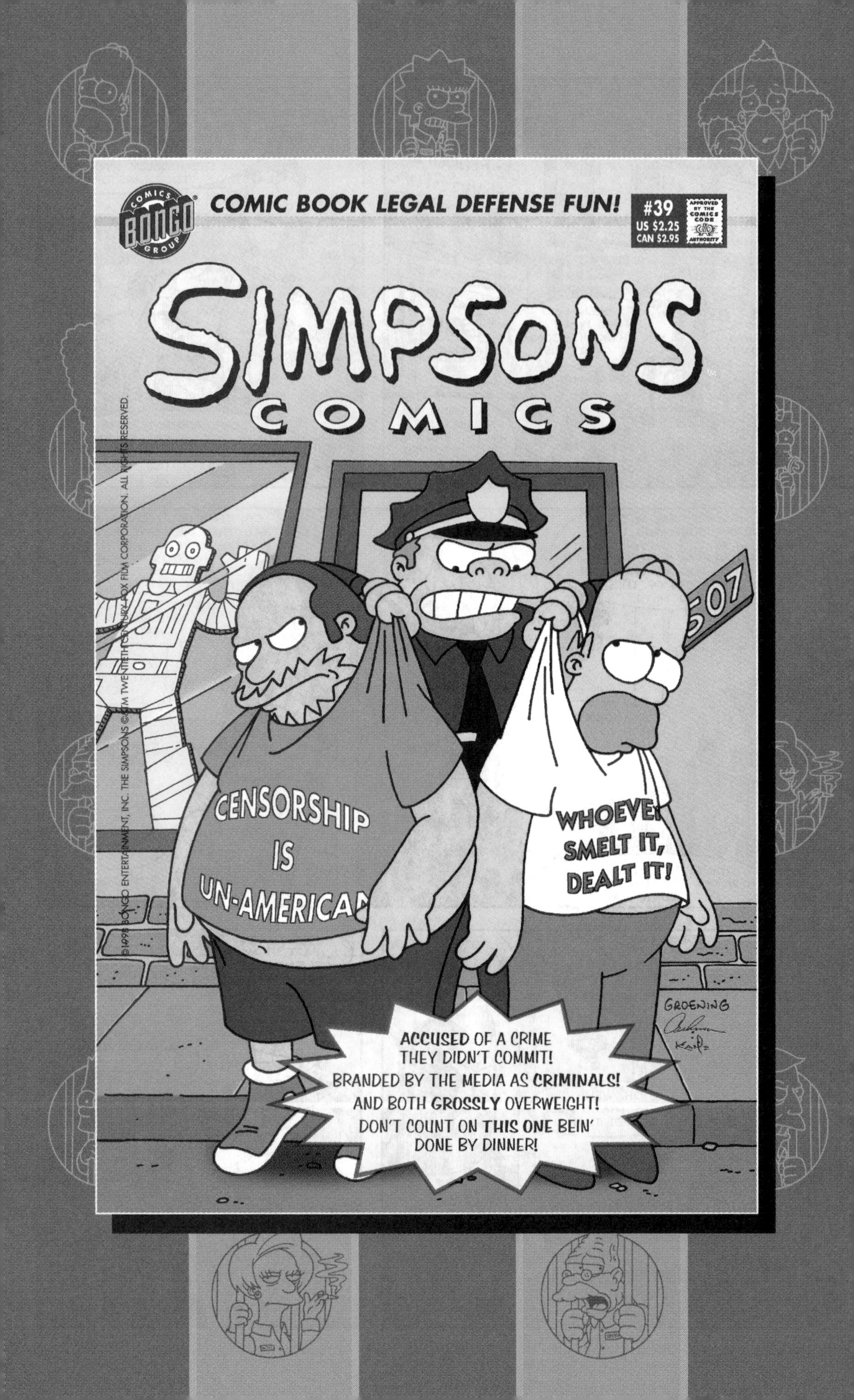
COMICS BONGO GROUP
COMIC BOOK LEGAL DEFENSE FUN!
#39
US $2.25
CAN $2.95
APPROVED BY THE COMICS CODE AUTHORITY
SIMPSONS
COMICS
©1998 BONGO ENTERTAINMENT, INC. THE SIMPSONS ©&TM TWENTIETH CENTURY FOX FILM CORPORATION. ALL RIGHTS RESERVED.
507
CENSORSHIP IS UN-AMERICAN
WHOEVER SMELT IT, DEALT IT!
GROENING
ACCUSED OF A CRIME THEY DIDN'T COMMIT!
BRANDED BY THE MEDIA AS CRIMINALS!
AND BOTH GROSSLY OVERWEIGHT!
DON'T COUNT ON THIS ONE BEIN' DONE BY DINNER!

IF MY CALCULATIONS ARE CORRECT, THIS KEY I'VE TIED TO THE END OF MY KITE SHOULD ACT AS A CONDUCTOR, DRAWING LIGHTNING TO IT...
...AND THUS, DESTROYING MY ARCHENEMY.
Sense and Censorability
SHA-KRAAK!
KITE-EATING TREE, I'LL SEE YOU IN HELL!!!
BWAH-HAH-HAH-HAAAAA!!!!
SCRIPT SCOTT M. GIMPLE
PENCILS PHIL ORTIZ
INKS TIM BAVINGTON
LETTERS JEANNINE BLACK
COLORS NATHAN KANE
EDITS BILL MORRISON
STAR WITNESS MATT GROENING

BENJAMIN FRANKLIN:
BIG BAD MUTHA OF INVENTION
...AND THAT'S HOW BENJAMIN FRANKLIN INVENTED ELECTRICITY. HE WENT ON TO INVENT OTHER USEFUL STUFF LIKE THE ODOMETER AND FRANCE. HE ALSO--
BART.
YOU'RE NOT BUYIN' ANY OF THIS, ARE YOU?
I STOPPED LISTENING WHEN YOU CALLED HIM THE BENJSTER.
SOON...
DID YOU REALLY THINK YOU'D GET AWAY WITH IT, BART? THANKS TO YOU, YOUR CLASS NOW THINKS THAT BENJAMIN FRANKLIN WAS A VENGEFUL, TREE-HATING, GIANT-BELT-BUCKLE-WEARING, KITE-WIELDING MANIAC! AND MY CONTACTS TELL ME THAT YOU'RE SPREADING A RUMOR THAT DAVY CROCKETT WORE A JAUNTILY-ASKEW BOWLER INSTEAD OF A COONSKIN CAP!
WELL, NO MORE! YOU SHALL PREPARE ANOTHER WELL-RESEARCHED REPORT ON THE HISTORICAL FIGURE OF YOUR CHOICE--EXCLUDING THE MAN WHO INVENTED THE TOILET.
THOMAS J. CRAPPER?
I KNOW WHO INVENTED THE TOILET, SIMPSON!!
YOU WILL DELIVER AN ORAL PRESENTATION IN FRONT OF THE ENTIRE SCHOOL NEXT WEEK AT OUR MONTHLY "WHAT BART DID WRONG AND WHY YOU SHOULDN'T DO IT" ASSEMBLY.

AND, SO YOU SHALL NEVER FORGET YOUR HISTORICAL TRANSGRESSION, YOU WILL PREPARE AND DELIVER SAID REPORT WITH YOUR FATHER...
HOMER J. SIMPSON!
I HAVE TO DO WHAT?
HOMER, YOU GOTTA WEAR A RADIATION SUIT WHEN YOU GO INTO THE CORE.
ANGER!
SECTOR 7-G
LENNY, THAT'S JUST A GUIDELINE.
RIIIING!
YEEEELLO. WHAT IS IT BOY? I HAVE TO DO WHAT?
WELL, CAN WE DO THE GUY WHO INVENTED THE TOILET?
D'OH.
LATER...
WHAT'RE WE GONNA DO? WHAT'RE WE GONNA DO? I DON'T KNOW HISTORY! I DON'T EVEN KNOW WHAT FREAKIN' COUNTRY WE'RE IN ANYMORE! THE UNITED STATES? AMERICA? LAND O' LAKES?
I DON'T WANNA LOOK AT BOOKS! I DON'T WANNA LOOK AT BOOKS! I CAN'T BREATHE!
UNCLE DAD'S SOUTHERN-STYLE CARAMEL TUB
Now with ice cream!
DAD, I KNOW WHAT YOU'RE GOING THROUGH, BUT YOU CAN'T PANIC. WHAT WE HAVE TO DO IS TAKE OUR MIND OFF OF IT. EASE INTO THE WORK...

COMING THIS JANUARY, THE MOST ANTICIPATED NEW CRIME SHOW OF THE MIDSEASON...
I'M THE BOOTY DETECTIVE AND I DETECT *BOOT-TAY!*
THE BOOTY DETECTIVE! ONLY ON FOX.
BASH!
GIVE IT UP, FLANDERS! WE *KNOW* YOU HAVE THE MICROCHIP--
WHY ELSE WOULD YOU HAVE CALLED US UP, TOLD US YOU STOLE IT, AND GIVEN US REALLY GOOD DIRECTIONS TO YOUR HOUSE?
SQUISHEE PAILS
SQUISHEE PAILS
RUSSIAN BEDPANS
46 KOUNT
THUDD!
WHAMM!
PUNCH!!
VIRTUA KIDNEY PUNCHER 5D
BIFF!!
HAPPY!!
"TAKE ME TO YOUR COMIC BOOKS & BASEBALL CARDS"
ONE MORE STOP, HOME-BOY. THEN WE HUNKER DOWN.
OPEN
507
Yes! We buy Micronauts!
BUT I DON'T WANNA HUNKER...

SOON...
WHAT IS THAT?
THAT IS MY "ADULTS ONLY" SECTION.
SO UNLESS YOU ARE A FULLY-GROWN STARFLEET OFFICER WHO WAS INVOLVED IN SOME SORT OF TRANSPORTER ACCIDENT THAT REMARKABLY DE-AGED YOU, STAY AWAY.
:SIGH:
FOR YOUR INFORMATION, IT IS ONE OF SPRINGFIELD'S MANY, MANY SURPLUS VOTING BOOTHS, WHICH I PURCHASED AT A CITY AUCTION.
ADULTS ONLY!
I WAS GOING TO USE IT TO HOLD A VOTE TO DETERMINE WHO WOULD WIN A BATTLE BETWEEN THE DESAAD AND GARGAMEL...
...BUT THEN I REALIZED THAT IT COULD BE OF BETTER USE AS A SANCTUARY FOR THE DISCRIMINATING, MATURE PATRONS OF THIS COMIC BOOK STORE.
ADULTS ONLY!
OOOOH! CLASSICS ILLUSTRATED'S LADY CHATTERLY'S LOVER! OOOH! THE ADVENTURES OF CLEAVAGE GIRL! OOOH! HEY-- WAITAMINUTE!
THIS ONE'S ABOUT THOMAS JEFFERSON. HE'S NOT ADULTS ONLY! HE'S NEVER BEEN ADULTS ONLY!
ADULTS ONLY!
HISTRIONIK COMICS
YOU ARE HOLDING IN YOUR HAND ISSUE TWENTY-EIGHT OF HISTRIONIK COMICS, THE COMIC BOOK THAT AMALGAMATES HISTORY WITH BONE-CHILLING HORROR. I BELIEVE THE TITLE OF THIS MONTH'S STORY IS "I, THOMAS JEFFERSON, CANNIBAL!" IT IS FOR MATURE READERS ONLY.
THOMAS JEFFERSON WAS A CANNIBAL?
LAST ISSUE, THEY REVEALED THAT BILLY CARTER WAS ACTUALLY A PEANUT FARMING WEREWOLF.
OOOOH!
#28
HISTRIONIK COMICS
I, THOMAS JEFFERSON, CANNIBAL!
We the People

"EUGENE V. DEBS AND HIS UNHOLY VAMPIRE UNION!" "BURIED ALIVE BY ELIZABETH CADY STANTON!" "ED MEESE--KING MAGGOT!" WE HIT THE JACKPOT, DAD! WE COULD DO EIGHT REPORTS ON THIS STUFF!
HISTRIONIK COMICS
OF COURSE IT'S A GOOD IDEA, MARGE! THE BOY HAS NEVER BEEN MORE INTERESTED IN SCHOOLWORK. THEY SHOULD HORRIFY ALL HIS SUBJECTS: MENTALLY-SCARRING MATH! SKIN-CRAWLING SCIENCE! HIGHLY-TRAUMATIC ENGLISH!
DAD, WHO ARE YOU TALKING TO?
OH, I THOUGHT THAT WAS MARGE. WELL, IT HAD TO BE SAID.
HEY, HOMER--WHY SHOULD WE STICK WITH JUST ONE HISTORICAL FIGURE? WE COULD DO A WHOLE OVERVIEW OF AMERICAN HISTORY!
HISTRIONIK COMICS
MR. PRESIDENT, I NEED YOUR SIGNATURE ON THESE—OH!
YOU HAVE DISCOVERED MY SECRET! FOR THAT, HUMAN, YOU SHALL DIE!
BEWARE THE BITTER STING— OF FDR... INVADER FROM ATLANTIS! THE TRUE STORY OF THE NEW DEAL!
GOOD IDEA, BOY. WE'LL SHOW 'EM THAT THERE ARE SMART SIMPSONS OTHER THAN LISA WITH HER BIG MATH AND ENGLISH BRAIN.
AUUUUGHHH!
BILLY BEER WAS ORIGINALLY BREWED TO TURN MILLIONS INTO WEREWOLVES!
OHMIGOD, OHMIGOD, OHMIGOD!! I'M AT RISK!
HISTRIONIK COMICS

...ALL I GOTTA REMEMBER IS THAT GEORGE WASHINGTON CHOPPED UP THE CHERRY SALESMAN...
ALTHOUGH SEEING YOU HUMILIATED BEFORE THE ENTIRE SCHOOL WOULD GIVE ME A GREAT SENSE OF ACCOMPLISHMENT, I'M GLAD TO SEE YOU'VE **PREPARED,** BART...
...AS I'VE INVITED SOME VERY **IMPORTANT** GUESTS.
"AFTER LISTENING TO THEIR CONCERNS AT THE CITY'S ANNUAL 'WHAT BART DID THIS YEAR AND HOW WE CAN MAKE SURE THOSE INCIDENTS NEVER REPEAT' CONFERENCE, I HAVE INVITED SUCH LUMINARIES AS;
"...THE GUFF-INTOLERANT **MAYOR QUIMBY**..."
"...OBSCENITY-SENSITIVES **MAUDE AND NED FLANDERS**..."
"...**REVEREND LOVEJOY** AND HIS ALARMIST WIFE, **HELEN**..."
"...YOUR FATHER'S PERPETUALLY-ANGRY BOSS **MR. BURNS** AND HIS DITHERING LICKSPITTLE, **WAYLON SMITHERS**..."
"...THE RELENTLESS LAWMAN **CHIEF WIGGUM**..."
"...AND SPRINGFIELD'S FAVORITE NO-NONSENSE JEWISH LEADER, **RABBI HYMAN KRUSTOFSKI**."
ARE WE SUPPOSED TO BE SCARED AND OR IMPRESSED? YOU TELL ALL THOSE POLITICAL AND RELIGIOUS LEADERS TO PREPARE TO HAVE THEIR BUTTS KICKED BY **HISTORY!**
DON'T
TAP
ME.
OKAY.

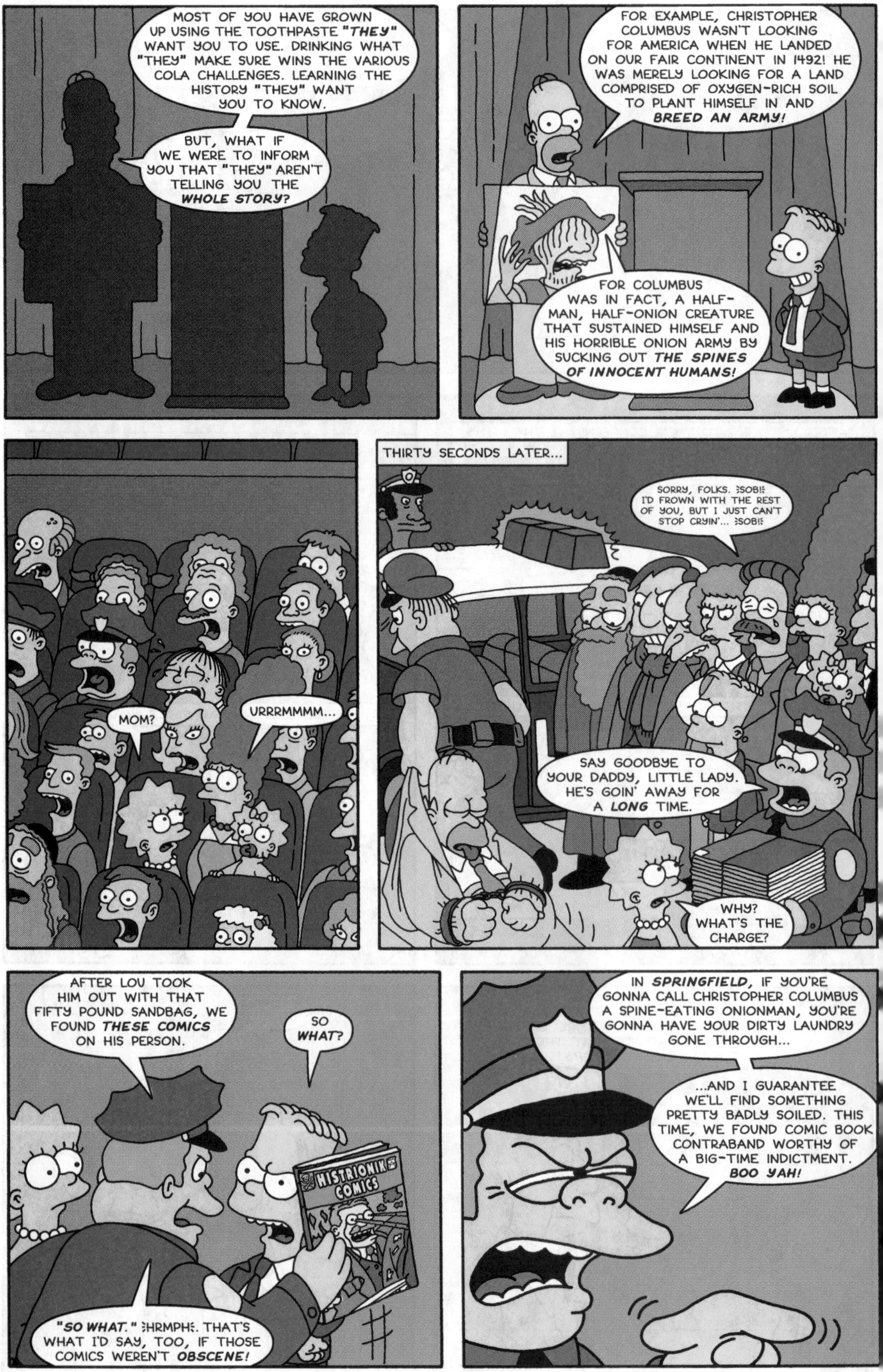
MOST OF YOU HAVE GROWN UP USING THE TOOTHPASTE "*THEY*" WANT YOU TO USE. DRINKING WHAT "THEY" MAKE SURE WINS THE VARIOUS COLA CHALLENGES. LEARNING THE HISTORY "THEY" WANT YOU TO KNOW.
BUT, WHAT IF WE WERE TO INFORM YOU THAT "THEY" AREN'T TELLING YOU THE ***WHOLE STORY?***
FOR EXAMPLE, CHRISTOPHER COLUMBUS WASN'T LOOKING FOR AMERICA WHEN HE LANDED ON OUR FAIR CONTINENT IN 1492! HE WAS MERELY LOOKING FOR A LAND COMPRISED OF OXYGEN-RICH SOIL TO PLANT HIMSELF IN AND ***BREED AN ARMY!***
FOR COLUMBUS WAS IN FACT, A HALF-MAN, HALF-ONION CREATURE THAT SUSTAINED HIMSELF AND HIS HORRIBLE ONION ARMY BY SUCKING OUT ***THE SPINES OF INNOCENT HUMANS!***
MOM?
URRRMMMM...
THIRTY SECONDS LATER...
SORRY, FOLKS. *SOB* I'D FROWN WITH THE REST OF YOU, BUT I JUST CAN'T STOP CRYIN'... *SOB*
SAY GOODBYE TO YOUR DADDY, LITTLE LADY. HE'S GOIN' AWAY FOR A ***LONG*** TIME.
WHY? WHAT'S THE CHARGE?
AFTER LOU TOOK HIM OUT WITH THAT FIFTY POUND SANDBAG, WE FOUND ***THESE COMICS*** ON HIS PERSON.
SO ***WHAT?***
HISTRIONIK COMICS
"***SO WHAT.***" *HRMPH*. THAT'S WHAT I'D SAY, TOO, IF THOSE COMICS WEREN'T ***OBSCENE!***
IN ***SPRINGFIELD,*** IF YOU'RE GONNA CALL CHRISTOPHER COLUMBUS A SPINE-EATING ONIONMAN, YOU'RE GONNA HAVE YOUR DIRTY LAUNDRY GONE THROUGH...
...AND I GUARANTEE WE'LL FIND SOMETHING PRETTY BADLY SOILED. THIS TIME, WE FOUND COMIC BOOK CONTRABAND WORTHY OF A BIG-TIME INDICTMENT. ***BOO YAH!***

OKAY! OKAY! I ADMIT IT! I'M THE ONE THAT TOOK THE WARHEAD FROM THE SPRINGFIELD MUSEUM'S NUCLEAR EXHIBIT!
I NEEDED IT IN CASE FLANDERS EVER WANTED TO START SOMETHING. IT'S HIDDEN IN--
SIMPSON, WE'RE TALKING ABOUT SOMETHING SERIOUS, HERE! WE TALKING ABOUT NAUGHTY, NAUGHTY FUNNYBOOKS!
KILL BART!! ~BOB
WHAH? COMIC BOOKS? YOU DRAGGED ME IN BECAUSE OF MY COMIC BOOKS?
UH, LOU? THEY HAVE STICKERS THAT SAY, "FROM THE LIBRARY OF HOMER SIMPSON."
SO, THEY ARE YOURS.
BUT I BOUGHT THEM FOR ME AND THE BOY.
YOU SHOWED THESE TO YOUR SON?
SURE, HE EXPLAINED ALL THE STUFF I DIDN'T UNDERSTAND, LIKE HOW GIANT LEECHES CAN TAKE ON HUMAN FORMS.
SIMPSON! YOU'RE LOOKING AT 180 YEARS HERE, EASY! PURCHASING OBSCENE MATERIAL! TRANSPORTING OBSCENE MATERIAL! PUBLICLY READING OBSCENE MATERIAL! BAGGING AND BOARDING OBSCENE MATERIAL IN THE HOPES THAT IT WILL GO UP IN VALUE!
NOW WHERE DID YOU GET THESE THINGS?
THAT WEIRD PLACE WITH THE THING IN THE WINDOW.
LET'S ROLL, LOU.

PIZZA
HOT
EVERYBODY OUT EXCEPT THE FAT GUY!
STAR WARS
OH, UH... I MEANT THE FAT GUY IN CHARGE. YOU FAT PEOPLE ARE FREE TO GO... THAT MEANS YOU, COMMANDER.
THAT WOULD BE CAPTAIN.
GENTLEMEN, GENTLEMEN. PLEASE. I ASSURE YOU, THERE ARE ENOUGH REAL-SWEATING SIPOWICZ DOLLS TO GO AROUND. THERE IS NO NEED TO--
HANDS UP, FUNNYMAN. YOU'RE GOING DOWNTOWN-- YOU, YOUR PIZZA, AND YOUR FOUR-COLOR SMUT.
FOR YOUR INFORMATION, A GREAT DEAL OF IT IS IN BLACK AND WHITE. THE REMAINING BOOKS ARE COLORED IN A STATE-OF-THE-ART MIRAWEB PROCESS--
PIZZA
SAVE IT FOR THE JUDGE, DUNGEONMASTER.
TURN THIS PLACE UPSIDE DOWN, FELLAS. WE NEED TO FIND MORE EVIDENCE AND THIS MONTH'S ISSUE OF "BETTY AND VERONICA" FOR THE CHIEF. APPARENTLY, THEY'RE HAVING SOME SORT OF ROMANTIC TROUBLE WITH ARCHIE.
OH GOOD LORD, NO!
NEW COMICS
BATMAN
RADIOACTIVE MAN
ACTION COMICS

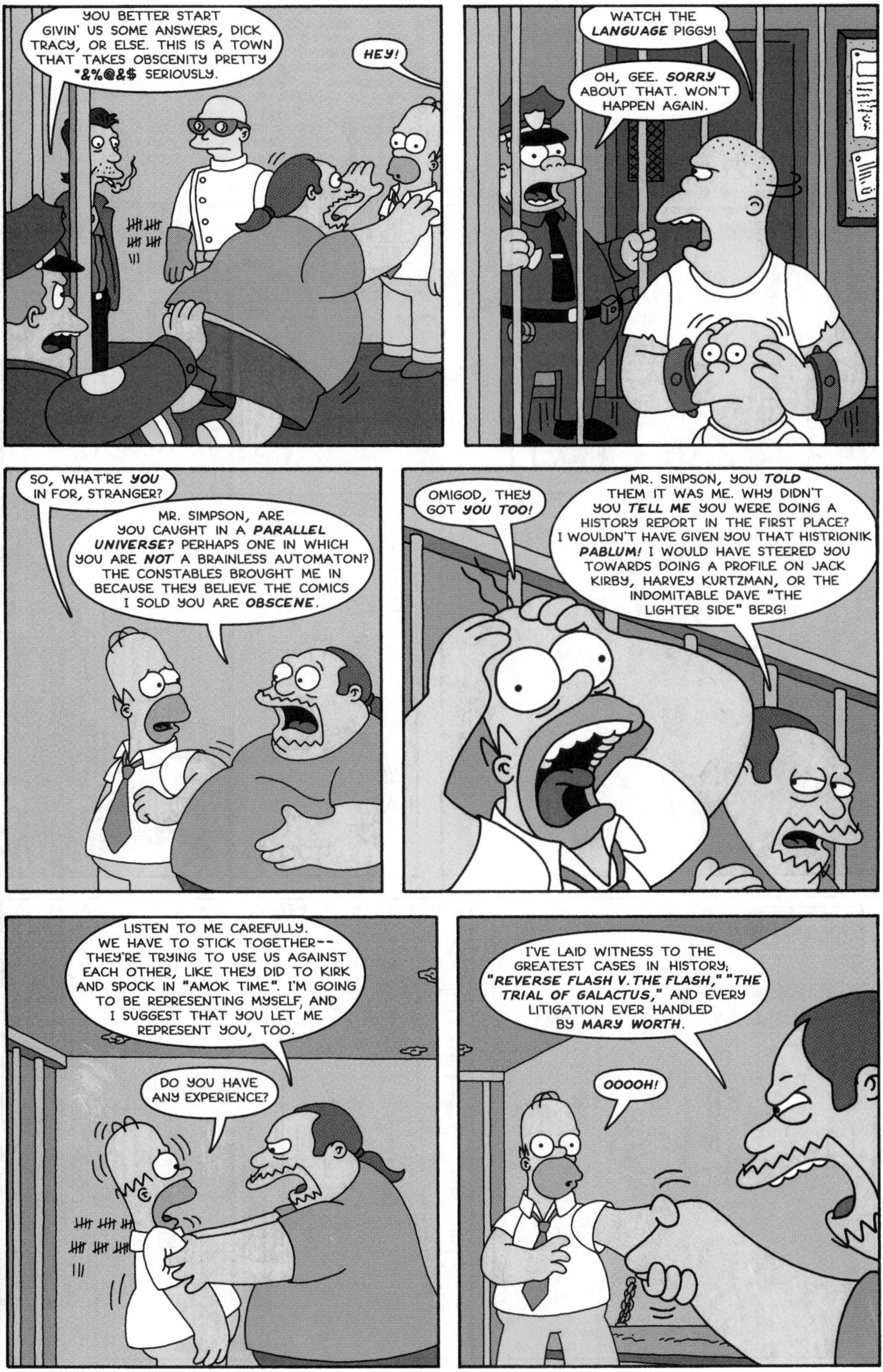
YOU BETTER START GIVIN' US SOME ANSWERS, DICK TRACY, OR ELSE. THIS IS A TOWN THAT TAKES OBSCENITY PRETTY *&%@&$ SERIOUSLY.
HEY!
WATCH THE LANGUAGE PIGGY!
OH, GEE. SORRY ABOUT THAT. WON'T HAPPEN AGAIN.
SO, WHAT'RE YOU IN FOR, STRANGER?
MR. SIMPSON, ARE YOU CAUGHT IN A PARALLEL UNIVERSE? PERHAPS ONE IN WHICH YOU ARE NOT A BRAINLESS AUTOMATON? THE CONSTABLES BROUGHT ME IN BECAUSE THEY BELIEVE THE COMICS I SOLD YOU ARE OBSCENE.
OMIGOD, THEY GOT YOU TOO!
MR. SIMPSON, YOU TOLD THEM IT WAS ME. WHY DIDN'T YOU TELL ME YOU WERE DOING A HISTORY REPORT IN THE FIRST PLACE? I WOULDN'T HAVE GIVEN YOU THAT HISTRIONIK PABLUM! I WOULD HAVE STEERED YOU TOWARDS DOING A PROFILE ON JACK KIRBY, HARVEY KURTZMAN, OR THE INDOMITABLE DAVE "THE LIGHTER SIDE" BERG!
LISTEN TO ME CAREFULLY. WE HAVE TO STICK TOGETHER-- THEY'RE TRYING TO USE US AGAINST EACH OTHER, LIKE THEY DID TO KIRK AND SPOCK IN "AMOK TIME". I'M GOING TO BE REPRESENTING MYSELF, AND I SUGGEST THAT YOU LET ME REPRESENT YOU, TOO.
DO YOU HAVE ANY EXPERIENCE?
I'VE LAID WITNESS TO THE GREATEST CASES IN HISTORY; "REVERSE FLASH V. THE FLASH," "THE TRIAL OF GALACTUS," AND EVERY LITIGATION EVER HANDLED BY MARY WORTH.
OOOOH!

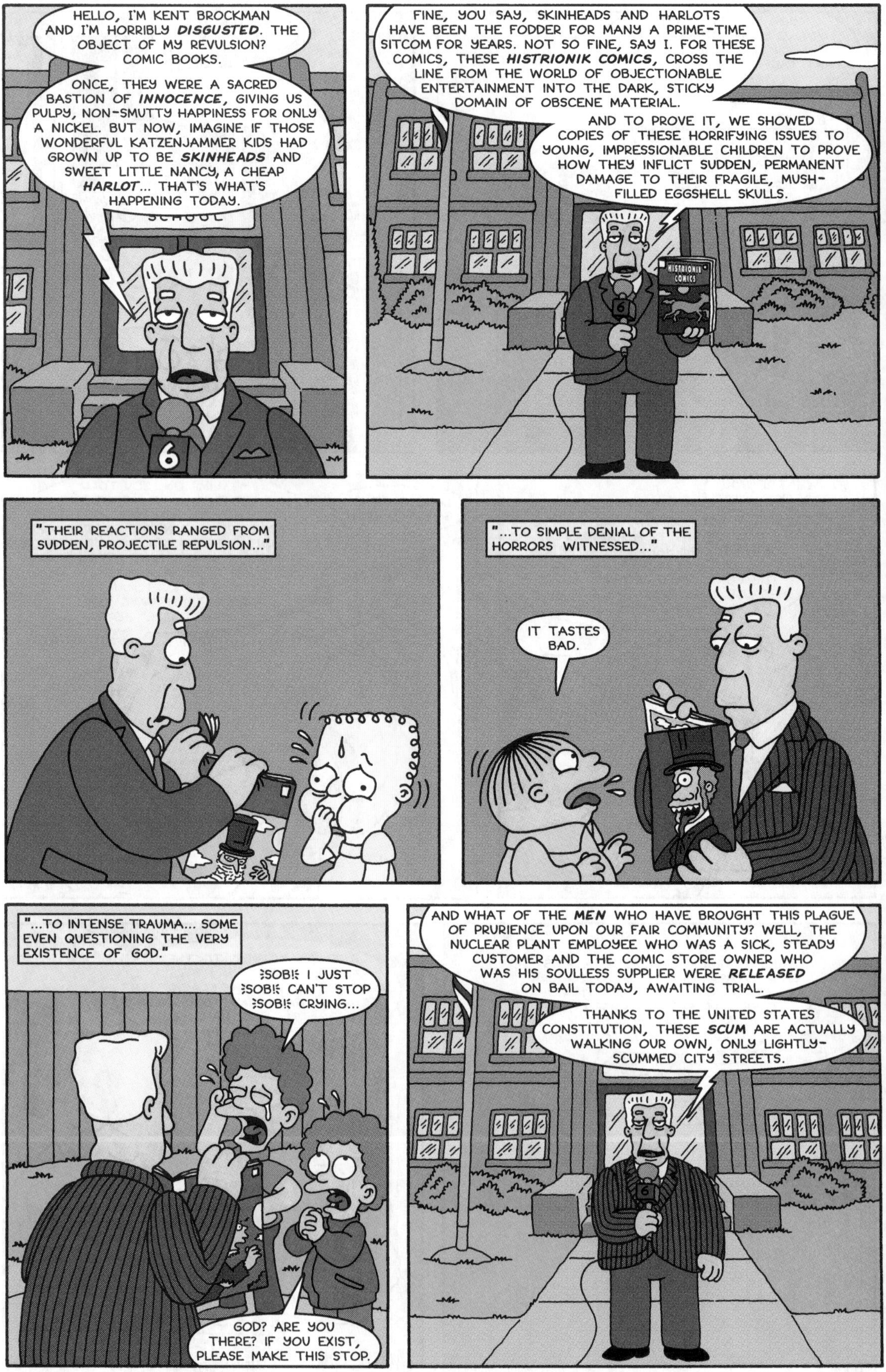
HELLO, I'M KENT BROCKMAN AND I'M HORRIBLY DISGUSTED. THE OBJECT OF MY REVULSION? COMIC BOOKS.
ONCE, THEY WERE A SACRED BASTION OF INNOCENCE, GIVING US PULPY, NON-SMUTTY HAPPINESS FOR ONLY A NICKEL. BUT NOW, IMAGINE IF THOSE WONDERFUL KATZENJAMMER KIDS HAD GROWN UP TO BE SKINHEADS AND SWEET LITTLE NANCY, A CHEAP HARLOT... THAT'S WHAT'S HAPPENING TODAY.
FINE, YOU SAY, SKINHEADS AND HARLOTS HAVE BEEN THE FODDER FOR MANY A PRIME-TIME SITCOM FOR YEARS. NOT SO FINE, SAY I. FOR THESE COMICS, THESE HISTRIONIK COMICS, CROSS THE LINE FROM THE WORLD OF OBJECTIONABLE ENTERTAINMENT INTO THE DARK, STICKY DOMAIN OF OBSCENE MATERIAL.
AND TO PROVE IT, WE SHOWED COPIES OF THESE HORRIFYING ISSUES TO YOUNG, IMPRESSIONABLE CHILDREN TO PROVE HOW THEY INFLICT SUDDEN, PERMANENT DAMAGE TO THEIR FRAGILE, MUSH-FILLED EGGSHELL SKULLS.
HISTRIONIK COMICS
"THEIR REACTIONS RANGED FROM SUDDEN, PROJECTILE REPULSION..."
"...TO SIMPLE DENIAL OF THE HORRORS WITNESSED..."
IT TASTES BAD.
"...TO INTENSE TRAUMA... SOME EVEN QUESTIONING THE VERY EXISTENCE OF GOD."
SOB! I JUST SOB! CAN'T STOP SOB! CRYING...
GOD? ARE YOU THERE? IF YOU EXIST, PLEASE MAKE THIS STOP.
AND WHAT OF THE MEN WHO HAVE BROUGHT THIS PLAGUE OF PRURIENCE UPON OUR FAIR COMMUNITY? WELL, THE NUCLEAR PLANT EMPLOYEE WHO WAS A SICK, STEADY CUSTOMER AND THE COMIC STORE OWNER WHO WAS HIS SOULLESS SUPPLIER WERE RELEASED ON BAIL TODAY, AWAITING TRIAL.
THANKS TO THE UNITED STATES CONSTITUTION, THESE SCUM ARE ACTUALLY WALKING OUR OWN, ONLY LIGHTLY-SCUMMED CITY STREETS.

I SIMPLY DON'T KNOW WHAT'S MORE PERVERTED; THESE HORRIBLE CONNOISSEURS OF TRIPEY YUCK OR OUR AMERICAN LEGAL SYSTEM. THIS IS KENT BROCKMAN, STILL DISGUSTED OUTSIDE OF SPRINGFIELD ELEMENTARY.
HOMER, YOU'VE BEEN OUT OF JAIL FOR ALMOST AN HOUR. YOU CAN TAKE THAT OFF NOW.
BUT IT'S JUST SO COMFORTABLE! THERE'S NO RESTRICTIVE WAISTLINE!
HOMER, I DON'T GET IT. WHAT DID WE DO WRONG?
CLICK!
BUFFY--SLAY IT! SLAY IT NOW! OH, PLEASE HURRY! THERE'S A SALE AT STRUCTURE!
WELL, KIDS, WHAT I DID WAS PURCHASE EIGHTEEN COMIC BOOKS THAT THE GOVERNMENT THINKS ARE TOO DISGUSTING TO BE READ BY ANY LIVING THING.
WAIT; YOU'RE SAYING THAT I COULD WRITE SOME WORDS AND DRAW SOME PICTURES SO GROSS THAT IT'D BE A CRIME TO LOOK AT THEM?
UH-HUH.
CLICK!
ALLY, YOU CAN'T ASK HIM OUT!
HE'S A FEDERAL JUDGE ABOUT TO SEND YOUR CLIENT TO THE ELECTRIC CHAIR!
SKRITCH SKRITCH
UH-HUH... I DON'T THINK HE'S WEARING ANYTHING UNDER THAT ROBE EXCEPT THOSE REALLY NICE ITALIAN SHOES.
HOW 'BOUT THIS?
NO.
THIS?
NO.
THIS?
NO.
FLIP FLIP FLIP
THIS?
WE HAVE A WINNER! NOW, THAT'S THE KIND OF STUFF THAT SENT ME TO THE BIG HOUSE!

DAD, THE FIRST AMENDMENT OF THE UNITED STATES CONSTITUTION SAYS THAT CONGRESS SHALL MAKE NO LAW ABRIDGING THE FREEDOM OF SPEECH OR FREEDOM OF THE PRESS.
IT WAS YOUR **CONSTITUTIONAL RIGHT** TO BUY THOSE GHASTLY COMICS JUST AS IT'S BART'S RIGHT TO DRAW THIS...
GAAAAURRRK.
YES, THAT IS CORRECT. HIS ***RIGHT***. AND PERHAPS THEY ALLOW YOU TO ACTUALLY EXERCISE THIS RIGHT SOMEWHERE NEAR THE PLANET QUORSHAN-8.
WHO--
I AM THE PROPRIETOR OF THE ***ANDROID'S DUNGEON***, AND I AM HERE TO DISCUSS ***LEGAL STRATEGY*** WITH MY CO-DEFENDANT.
BUT HOW DID YOU GET IN?
AFTER USING A MOTHER BOX TO FLING MYSELF INTO THE ***FUTURE***, I ACCESSED RECORDS OF WHAT TRANSPIRED IN OUR TRIAL. I THEN SPENT SOME TIME WORKING FOR THE FEDERATION, GATHERING EXPERIENCE WHILE TRYING COURT-MARTIALS.
FINALLY, I USED AN EXPERIMENTAL PROCEDURE ON THE TRANSPORTER ROOM'S SENSOR ARRAY, ALLOWING ME TO BE BEAMED BACK HERE, INTO YOUR LIVING ROOM.
OKAY, YOUR FRONT DOOR WAS AJAR. SO UM, LET'S GET TO WORK.
OOOH! I JUST ***LOVE*** WHAT YOU DID WITH YOUR ***PRISON UNIFORM!***
I JUST MADE SOME MINOR ALTERATIONS. THIS IS THE MOST COMFORTABLE PIECE OF CLOTHING I'VE EVER WORN! THERE'S NO RESTRICTIVE WAISTLINE.
SPRINGFIELD JAIL

SINCE THE DAWN OF TIME, GOVERNMENT HAS HATED COMIC BOOK SHOPS. NOT ONLY DO COMIC BOOKS HELP FOSTER A THIRST FOR TRUTH AND JUSTICE, BUT THEY ARE ALSO A FORUM FOR IMPORTANT IDEAS, SUCH AS THE NOW-CLASSIC YARN, RADIOACTIVE MAN VS. THE LIVING BONG.
HISTRIONIK COMICS
SPRINGFIELD JAIL
SPRINGFIELD HAS BEEN AN ESPECIALLY INHOSPITABLE ENVIRONMENT FOR THE MEDIUM. AFTER THIS ONE-PANEL GAG WAS PUBLISHED IN THE SPRINGFIELD SHOPPER, MAYOR QUIMBY WENT ON TO BAN ALL POLITICAL CARTOONS.
IN 1980, WHEN A YOUNG TYKE CHOKED ON A COPY OF SECRET WARS #4, THE CITY SHUT DOWN "THE GEEKERY", SAYING THAT COMICS WERE UNSAFE FOR THE READING PUBLIC.
TWO YEARS LATER, "SEQUENTIAL ART'S" WAS RUN OUT OF BUSINESS BECAUSE THE CITY THOUGHT THAT THE FLASH WAS ABOUT A HERO THAT BESTED HIS FOES BY EXPOSING HIMSELF.
DIAMOND JOE: THE MUSICAL
Wine, women, and wrong (doing)!
Turns out DIAMOND JOE was a CUBIC ZIRCONIA.
CLOSED BY ORDER OF THE CITY
The Geekery
Springfield Shopper
Super-nudie nightmare nixed
THEY THINK THEY CAN PUSH US AROUND TO FURTHER THEIR OWN TWISTED AGENDAS AND OPEN RETAIL SPACE FOR COFFEEHOUSES THAT BESMIRCH THE NAMES OF BELOVED BATTLESTAR GALACTICA CHARACTERS.
ONE BY ONE, MY COMPETITION HAS BEEN CLOSED DOWN--NOT BY MY SUPERIOR RACKING AND MARKETING, BUT BY A TECHNOCRATIC, OPPRESSIVE GOVERNMENT. I KNEW ONE DAY, THEY WOULD COME AFTER ME. BUT I AM READY.
LIS, DAD IS THREE STEPS AWAY FROM THE STATE PEN! WE GOTTA DO SOMETHING.
BART, THIS ISN'T LIKE FINDING A BOOK OF SPELLS TO REVERSE A ZOMBIE CURSE OR READING THROUGH ANCIENT JUDAIC TEXTS TO FIND ARGUMENTS TO JUSTIFY CLOWNING-- THIS IS OBSCENITY LAW. IT'S GOING TO TAKE SOME TIME!
THE LAWYERS, THE GOVERNMENT OFFICIALS, THAT HORRIBLE "UP WITH PEOPLE" ORGANIZATION--I KNOW THEIR TACTICS. THEY ARE A SUPERSTITIOUS, COWARDLY LOT, FRAGGIN' BASTICHES ONE AND ALL. THEY DON'T JUST FIGHT IN THE COURTROOM, AND NEITHER SHOULD WE!
MR. SIMPSON...
...PLEASE GIVE MY FEDERATION TORCH BACK AND TURN THE LIGHT BACK ON!
OKAY.
OUR FIRST PRIORITY IS SPIN. IF WE HAVE ANY HOPE OF WINNING THIS CASE, WE HAVE TO MANIPULATE THE MEDIA, WHICH HAS PORTRAYED US AS MONSTERS...

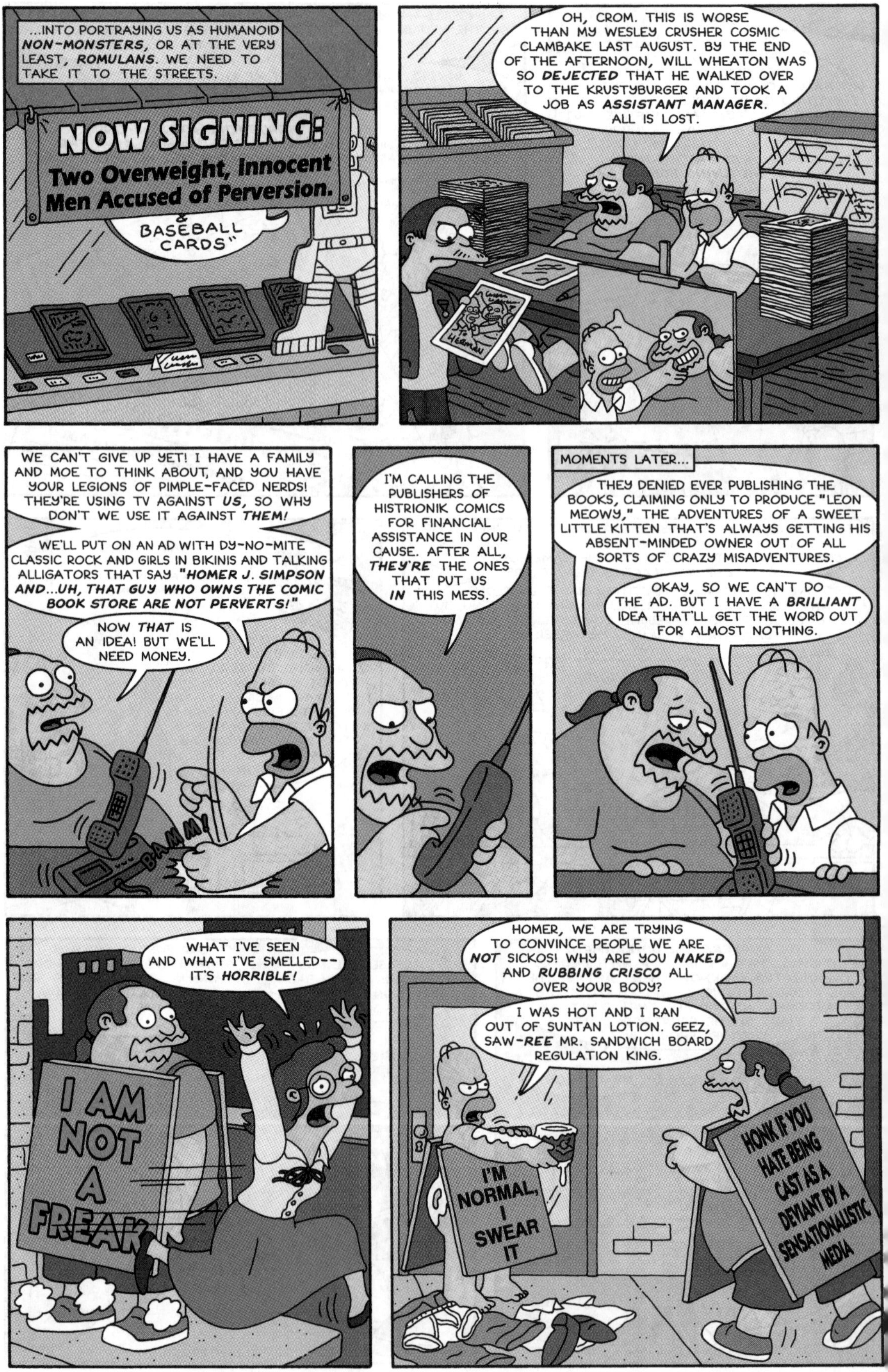
...INTO PORTRAYING US AS HUMANOID *NON-MONSTERS*, OR AT THE VERY LEAST, *ROMULANS*. WE NEED TO TAKE IT TO THE STREETS.
NOW SIGNING: Two Overweight, Innocent Men Accused of Perversion.
& BASEBALL CARDS"
OH, CROM. THIS IS WORSE THAN MY WESLEY CRUSHER COSMIC CLAMBAKE LAST AUGUST. BY THE END OF THE AFTERNOON, WILL WHEATON WAS SO *DEJECTED* THAT HE WALKED OVER TO THE KRUSTYBURGER AND TOOK A JOB AS *ASSISTANT MANAGER*. ALL IS LOST.
WE CAN'T GIVE UP YET! I HAVE A FAMILY AND MOE TO THINK ABOUT, AND YOU HAVE YOUR LEGIONS OF PIMPLE-FACED NERDS! THEY'RE USING TV AGAINST *US*, SO WHY DON'T WE USE IT AGAINST *THEM!*
WE'LL PUT ON AN AD WITH DY-NO-MITE CLASSIC ROCK AND GIRLS IN BIKINIS AND TALKING ALLIGATORS THAT SAY *"HOMER J. SIMPSON AND...UH, THAT GUY WHO OWNS THE COMIC BOOK STORE ARE NOT PERVERTS!"*
NOW *THAT* IS AN IDEA! BUT WE'LL NEED MONEY.
BAMM!
I'M CALLING THE PUBLISHERS OF HISTRIONIK COMICS FOR FINANCIAL ASSISTANCE IN OUR CAUSE. AFTER ALL, *THEY'RE* THE ONES THAT PUT US *IN* THIS MESS.
MOMENTS LATER...
THEY DENIED EVER PUBLISHING THE BOOKS, CLAIMING ONLY TO PRODUCE "LEON MEOWY," THE ADVENTURES OF A SWEET LITTLE KITTEN THAT'S ALWAYS GETTING HIS ABSENT-MINDED OWNER OUT OF ALL SORTS OF CRAZY MISADVENTURES.
OKAY, SO WE CAN'T DO THE AD. BUT I HAVE A *BRILLIANT* IDEA THAT'LL GET THE WORD OUT FOR ALMOST NOTHING.
WHAT I'VE SEEN AND WHAT I'VE SMELLED-- IT'S *HORRIBLE!*
I AM NOT A FREAK
HOMER, WE ARE TRYING TO CONVINCE PEOPLE WE ARE *NOT* SICKOS! WHY ARE YOU *NAKED* AND *RUBBING CRISCO* ALL OVER YOUR BODY?
I WAS HOT AND I RAN OUT OF SUNTAN LOTION. GEEZ, SAW-*REE* MR. SANDWICH BOARD REGULATION KING.
I'M NORMAL, I SWEAR IT
HONK IF YOU HATE BEING CAST AS A DEVIANT BY A SENSATIONALISTIC MEDIA

GOOD MORNING EVERYONE, COURT IS NOW IN SESSION. BEFORE WE START, I'D LIKE TO THANK "SPRINGFIELDERS FOR CHILDREN AND FAMILIES AND WELL-BEHAVED PETS" FOR THE WONDERFUL FRUIT BASKET THEY SENT ME THIS MORNING.
HANG 'EM HIGH, YOUR HONOR!
S.F.C.A.F. A.W.B.P
S.F.C.A.F. A.W.B.P
S.F.C.A.F. A.W.B.P
WELL, IT'S GOING TO BE UP TO THE JURY, BUT I'LL SEE WHAT I CAN DO. DEFENSE, BEGIN YOUR OPENING STATEMENT.
MR. SIMPSON, PREPARE TO BE DAZZLED.
SPRINGFIELD JAIL
PUNY HUMANS, WHEN WILL YOU LEARN? HULK STRONGER THAN YOU. HULK SMARTER THAN YOU. HULK SMASH YOU.
OF COURSE, I AM NOT THE HULK, THE HULK IS THE TRUTH. BUT YOU ARE THE PUNY HUMANS. WHAT'S WORSE, YOU'RE PUNY HUMANS THAT HAVE DELUDED YOURSELVES INTO THINKING THAT YOU ARE FIT TO PASS JUDGMENT LIKE THE GUARDIANS OF THE GALAXY, GALACTUS, OR EVEN, KLAATU!
ARE YOU ALL SO WITHOUT BIAS? AS IF YOU WERE SHIELDED FROM THIS WORLD BY YOUR OWN BACTA TANKS, SAFE AND SOUND FROM THE RANCORS AND YAMBARS OF INFLUENCE THAT SURELY CLOUD YOUR JUDGEMENT!
YOU ARE NOT IMPARTIAL DATAS, WATCHERS, OR EVEN BEYONDERS. YOU ARE SKRULLS, CYLONS, AND MEMBERS OF THE DRACONIAN EMPIRE, FLAWED IN DISPOSITIONS AND THOUGHT PATTERNS.
YOUR HONOR, I BELIEVE WE REQUIRE SOME SORT OF TRANSLATION.
DOES ANYONE SPEAK... THAT LANGUAGE HE JUST USED?
JOHWI'VAD MAMUGHLAH.
THAT WAS KLINGON FOR, "WE CAN TRANSLATE, YOUR HONOR."

...THEY SPOKE IN GOBBLEDY-GEEK ALL DAY, REFERRING TO ALIENS, SUPERHEROES, AND JAPANESE MONSTERS TO MAKE THEIR CONVOLUTED POINTS. THEIR REFERENCES TO THE HISTRIONIK COMIC BOOKS MADE SEVERAL JURORS PHYSICALLY ILL, AND HOMER SIMPSON, MISTAKING IT FOR A BATHROOM, RELIEVED HIMSELF IN THE JUROR'S COAT CLOSET.
WOULD YOU SAY IT'S NOT LOOKING GOOD FOR THE DEFENSE?
BART, I'VE LOOKED AT FEDERAL CASES RIGHT DOWN TO THE LOCAL LEVEL. I THINK WE'RE IN TROUBLE.
LISA, WHAT USE ARE SUPERIOR RESEARCH SKILLS AND A GREAT VOCABULARY IF YOU CAN'T SPRING YOUR DAD FROM AN OBSCENITY CHARGE?
I'D SAY THEY SHOULD PREPARE FOR PRISON LIFE.
I'D AGREE. THEY SHOULD SPEND THE NEXT FEW DAYS USING CIGARETTES AS CURRENCY, JUST TO GET THE HANG OF IT.
ALL THESE CASES--"DOG-EARED DAVE V. CALIFORNIA," "BATTLESTAR COMICBOOK-SHOPTICA V. TEXAS," AND "EVERY COMIC READER IN AMERICA V. OKLAHOMA"--RESULTED IN CONVICTIONS. THE DEFENDANTS JUST COULDN'T GET THE JURY TO STOP THINKING ABOUT THE SENSATIONAL ASPECTS OF THE CASE AND START THINKING ABOUT THE FIRST AMENDMENT.
JUR-EE?
JURY! THEY'RE THE PEOPLE WHO SIT IN THE JURY BOX AND DECIDE THE CASE.
OH. I JUST THOUGHT THOSE WERE THE PEOPLE WITH THE GOOD SEATS.
BART, THE FACT THAT EVERYONE IS ENTITLED UNDER LAW TO A SPEEDY TRIAL BEFORE A FAIR, IMPARTIAL JURY OF THEIR PEERS IS ONE OF THE MOST BASIC PRECEPTS OF AMERICAN LIFE! WHERE HAVE YOU BEEN DURING SOCIAL STUDIES CLASS?
READING COMICS, MOSTLY. JUST BE HAPPY I KNOW WHAT THE WORD "PEER" MEANS.
WAITAMINUTE...
MR. SIMPSON, THE TRIAL IS NOT GOING WELL. THE JUDGE DOESN'T LIKE US, THE JURY DOESN'T LIKE US, AND THE STENOGRAPHER HURLED HER MACHINE AT YOU DURING THE MIDDLE OF YOUR TESTIMONY. I THINK WE NEED A NEW STRATEGY. FORTUNATELY, I HAVE ONE.
SHE SAID IT SLIPPED.

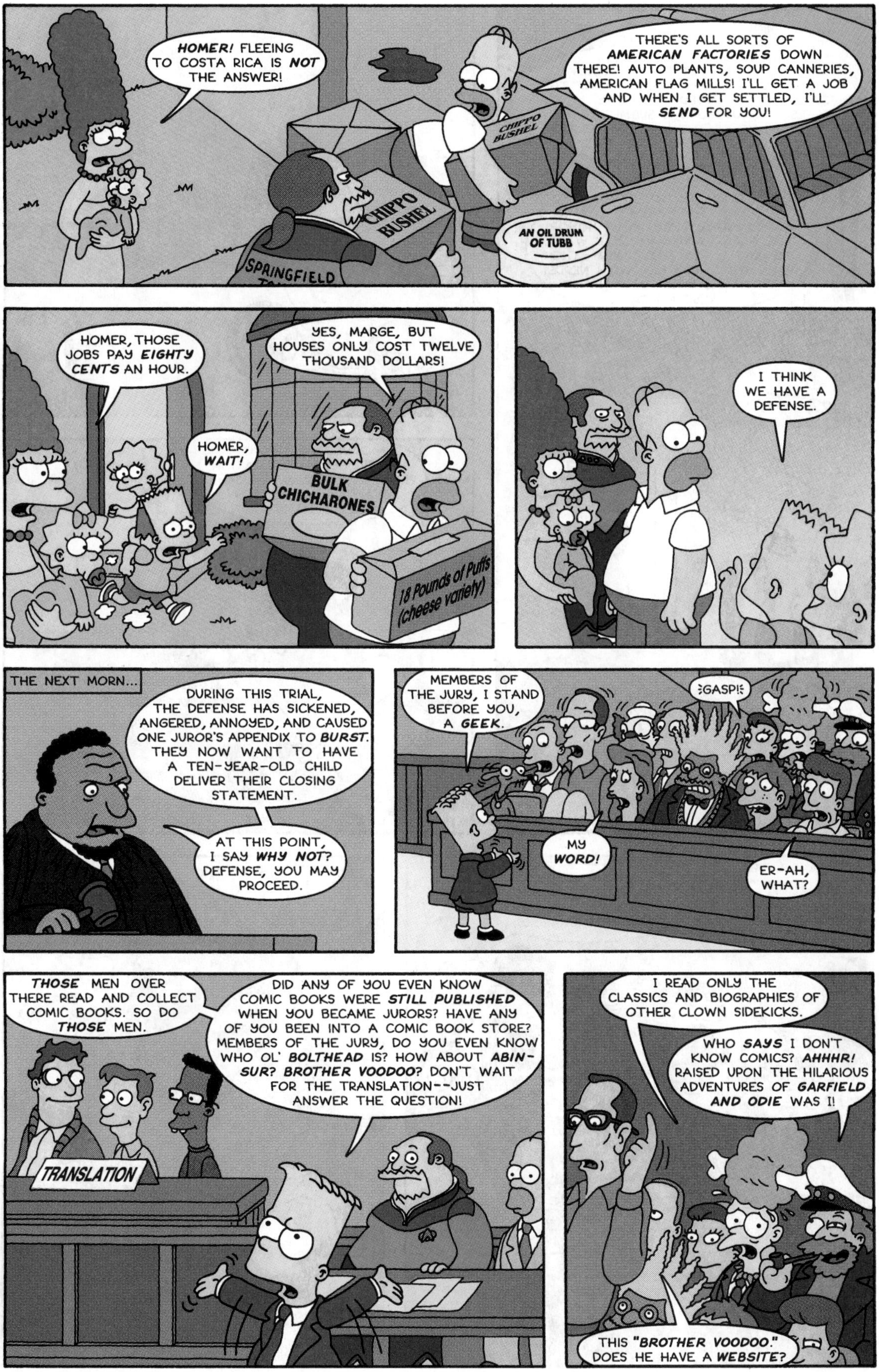
HOMER! FLEEING TO COSTA RICA IS NOT THE ANSWER!
THERE'S ALL SORTS OF AMERICAN FACTORIES DOWN THERE! AUTO PLANTS, SOUP CANNERIES, AMERICAN FLAG MILLS! I'LL GET A JOB AND WHEN I GET SETTLED, I'LL SEND FOR YOU!
CHIPPO BUSHEL
CHIPPO BUSHEL
AN OIL DRUM OF TUBB
SPRINGFIELD
HOMER, THOSE JOBS PAY EIGHTY CENTS AN HOUR.
YES, MARGE, BUT HOUSES ONLY COST TWELVE THOUSAND DOLLARS!
HOMER, WAIT!
BULK CHICHARONES
18 Pounds of Puffs (cheese variety)
I THINK WE HAVE A DEFENSE.
THE NEXT MORN...
DURING THIS TRIAL, THE DEFENSE HAS SICKENED, ANGERED, ANNOYED, AND CAUSED ONE JUROR'S APPENDIX TO BURST. THEY NOW WANT TO HAVE A TEN-YEAR-OLD CHILD DELIVER THEIR CLOSING STATEMENT.
AT THIS POINT, I SAY WHY NOT? DEFENSE, YOU MAY PROCEED.
MEMBERS OF THE JURY, I STAND BEFORE YOU, A GEEK.
GASP!
MY WORD!
ER-AH, WHAT?
THOSE MEN OVER THERE READ AND COLLECT COMIC BOOKS. SO DO THOSE MEN.
DID ANY OF YOU EVEN KNOW COMIC BOOKS WERE STILL PUBLISHED WHEN YOU BECAME JURORS? HAVE ANY OF YOU BEEN INTO A COMIC BOOK STORE? MEMBERS OF THE JURY, DO YOU EVEN KNOW WHO OL' BOLTHEAD IS? HOW ABOUT ABIN-SUR? BROTHER VOODOO? DON'T WAIT FOR THE TRANSLATION--JUST ANSWER THE QUESTION!
TRANSLATION
I READ ONLY THE CLASSICS AND BIOGRAPHIES OF OTHER CLOWN SIDEKICKS.
WHO SAYS I DON'T KNOW COMICS? AHHHR! RAISED UPON THE HILARIOUS ADVENTURES OF GARFIELD AND ODIE WAS I!
THIS "BROTHER VOODOO." DOES HE HAVE A WEBSITE?

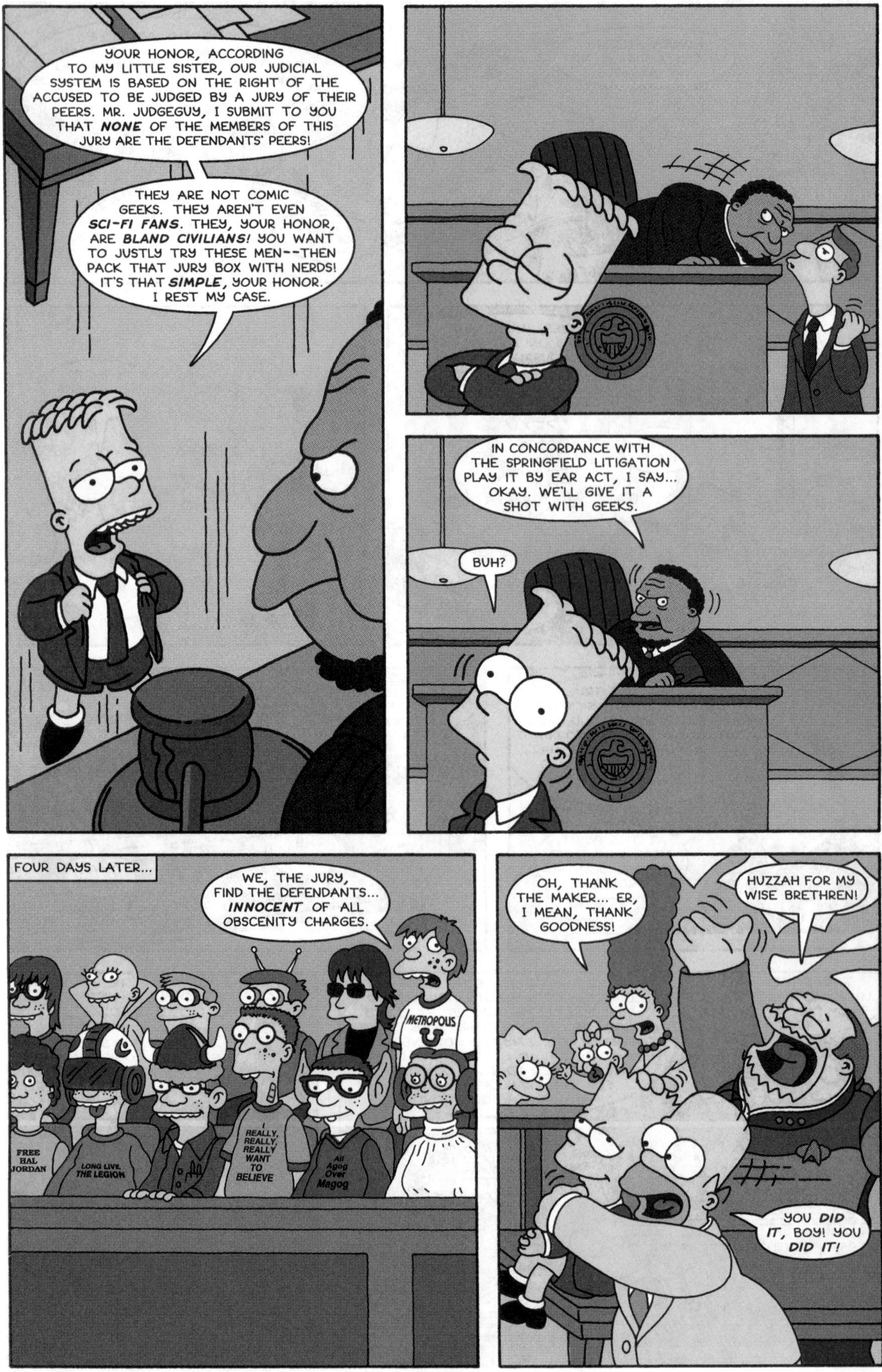
YOUR HONOR, ACCORDING TO MY LITTLE SISTER, OUR JUDICIAL SYSTEM IS BASED ON THE RIGHT OF THE ACCUSED TO BE JUDGED BY A JURY OF THEIR PEERS. MR. JUDGEGUY, I SUBMIT TO YOU THAT NONE OF THE MEMBERS OF THIS JURY ARE THE DEFENDANTS' PEERS!
THEY ARE NOT COMIC GEEKS. THEY AREN'T EVEN SCI-FI FANS. THEY, YOUR HONOR, ARE BLAND CIVILIANS! YOU WANT TO JUSTLY TRY THESE MEN--THEN PACK THAT JURY BOX WITH NERDS! IT'S THAT SIMPLE, YOUR HONOR. I REST MY CASE.
IN CONCORDANCE WITH THE SPRINGFIELD LITIGATION PLAY IT BY EAR ACT, I SAY... OKAY. WE'LL GIVE IT A SHOT WITH GEEKS.
BUH?
FOUR DAYS LATER...
WE, THE JURY, FIND THE DEFENDANTS... INNOCENT OF ALL OBSCENITY CHARGES.
METROPOLIS
FREE HAL JORDAN
LONG LIVE THE LEGION
I REALLY, REALLY, REALLY WANT TO BELIEVE
All Agog Over Magog
OH, THANK THE MAKER... ER, I MEAN, THANK GOODNESS!
HUZZAH FOR MY WISE BRETHREN!
YOU DID IT, BOY! YOU DID IT!

HOWEVER, THE JURY DID CHOOSE TO INFLICT ADDITIONAL CHARGES, WHICH, ALTHOUGH UNCONSTITUTIONAL, ARE PERMITTED ON SEVERAL FEDERATION PLANETS.
DEFENDANT ONE, PLEASE RISE.
METROPOLIS U
I REALLY, REALLY, REALLY WANT TO BELIEVE
HUH?
WHA?
WHOOZA?
WE FIND YOU GUILTY OF CONDESCENSION, COVER-CRINKLING, PRICE-GOUGING, USING HIGHLY ACIDIC BOARDS, SELLING COMICS SOILED BY BURRITO DRIPPINGS, RUINING THE ENDING TO THE "DEATH OF SUPERMAN," AND BRIBING THE MANAGER OF THE TOY AISLE AT TRY N' SAVE TO BUY UP ALL THE NEW "HIP-HOP YO! YO! YODA" ACTION FIGURES.
DEFENDANT TWO, WE FIND YOU GUILTY OF CALLING ***MAD MAGAZINE*** A COMIC BOOK, NAMING ***BATMAN & ROBIN*** AS YOUR FAVORITE OF THE MOVIE SERIES, AND, DURING THE COURSE OF THIS TRIAL, REPEATEDLY CALLING THE JURY BOX THE "NERD NOOK" AND GIVING ALL OF US WEDGIES.
FOR THESE TRESPASSES AGAINST OUR MOST SACRED BELIEFS WE SENTENCE BOTH OF YOU...
...TO ***PUBLIC HANGING!!***
AISLE 1000
GEEZ, IT'S HOT. I DON'T KNOW ABOUT ***YOU***, BUT I'M TAKING OFF MY PANTS.
TWO OVERWEIGHT MEN ACQUITTED OF OBSCENITY WELCOME YOU TO CLOSE ENCOUNTERS OF THE COMIC BOOK KIND IX
CONGO COMICS
EXIT
NOW SIGNING! COMIC BOOK LEGAL SCHOLAR Bart Simpson Room 7A-B
RARE!
SUPER RARE
THE END.

SIMPSONS
COMICS
BONGO COMICS GROUP
#40
US $2.50
CAN $3.50
APPROVED BY THE COMICS CODE AUTHORITY
©1998 BONGO ENTERTAINMENT, INC. THE SIMPSONS ©&TM TWENTIETH CENTURY FOX FILM CORPORATION. ALL RIGHTS RESERVED.
GROENING

SIDESHOW SIMPSONS
WELCOME TO FLANDERS COUNTRY
HEY BARNEY, GO FIND NED. I WANT HIM TO SEE ME SINK THE EIGHT BALL BEHIND MY BACK.
SCRIPT BILL MORRISON
PENCILS PHIL ORTIZ
INKS TIM BAVINGTON
LETTERS JEANNINE BLACK
COLORS NATHAN KANE
CUE CARD BOY MATT GROENING
8

HOMER SIMPSON! WHAT ARE YOU DING-DIDDLY DOING HERE? IT'S THREE O'CLOCK IN THE MORNING!
MOE HAD TO CLOSE UP THE BAR IN THE MIDDLE OF OUR GAME. LUCKY FOR US, I REMEMBERED THAT YOU HAD A BAR WITH A POOL TABLE TOO, AND YOUR PLACE NEVER CLOSES!
BUT MY DOOR WAS CLOSED--AND LOCKED! HOW DID YOU GET IN?
I'LL FIELD THAT QUESHTION. SHKELETON KEYS TO EVERY HOUSH IN TOWN!
SOON...
HOMER, I'M SURE THIS IS THE BEST IDEA YOU'VE EVER HAD, ≷YAWN≶ BUT CAN'T IT WAIT TILL MORNING?
BUT JUST THINK ABOUT IT, MARGE! OUR VERY OWN REC ROOM, JUST LIKE FLANDERS... RIGHT HERE IN OUR BASEMENT! WE'LL HAVE A POOL TABLE, AND A JUKEBOX...AND A BAR, MARGE! A BAR, COMPLETE WITH ONE OF THOSE CUTE LITTLE PLASTIC DRUNK GUYS WHO DROP THEIR PANTS AND SHOOT WHISKEY INTO YOUR GLASS!
WHERE ARE WE GOING?
JUST FOLLOW ME. I WANT TO SHOW YOU SOMETHING.
SEE THIS MESS? THERE'S NOT EVEN ROOM FOR A FOOSBALL GAME, MUCH LESS A BAR AND POOL TABLE. I WON'T EVEN THINK ABOUT LETTING YOU BUILD YOUR LITTLE CLUBHOUSE UNTIL THIS BASEMENT IS CLEANED OUT--STARTING WITH THAT OLMEC INDIAN HEAD!
BUT MARGE, THAT WAS A GIFT FROM MY BOSS. SUPPOSE HE COMES OVER.
HE CAN'T EVEN REMEMBER YOUR NAME! WHAT MAKES YOU THINK HE'S GOING TO DROP IN FOR A VISIT?
I'M SORRY HOMER, BUT IF YOU WANT A REC ROOM, THAT THING HAS TO GO.

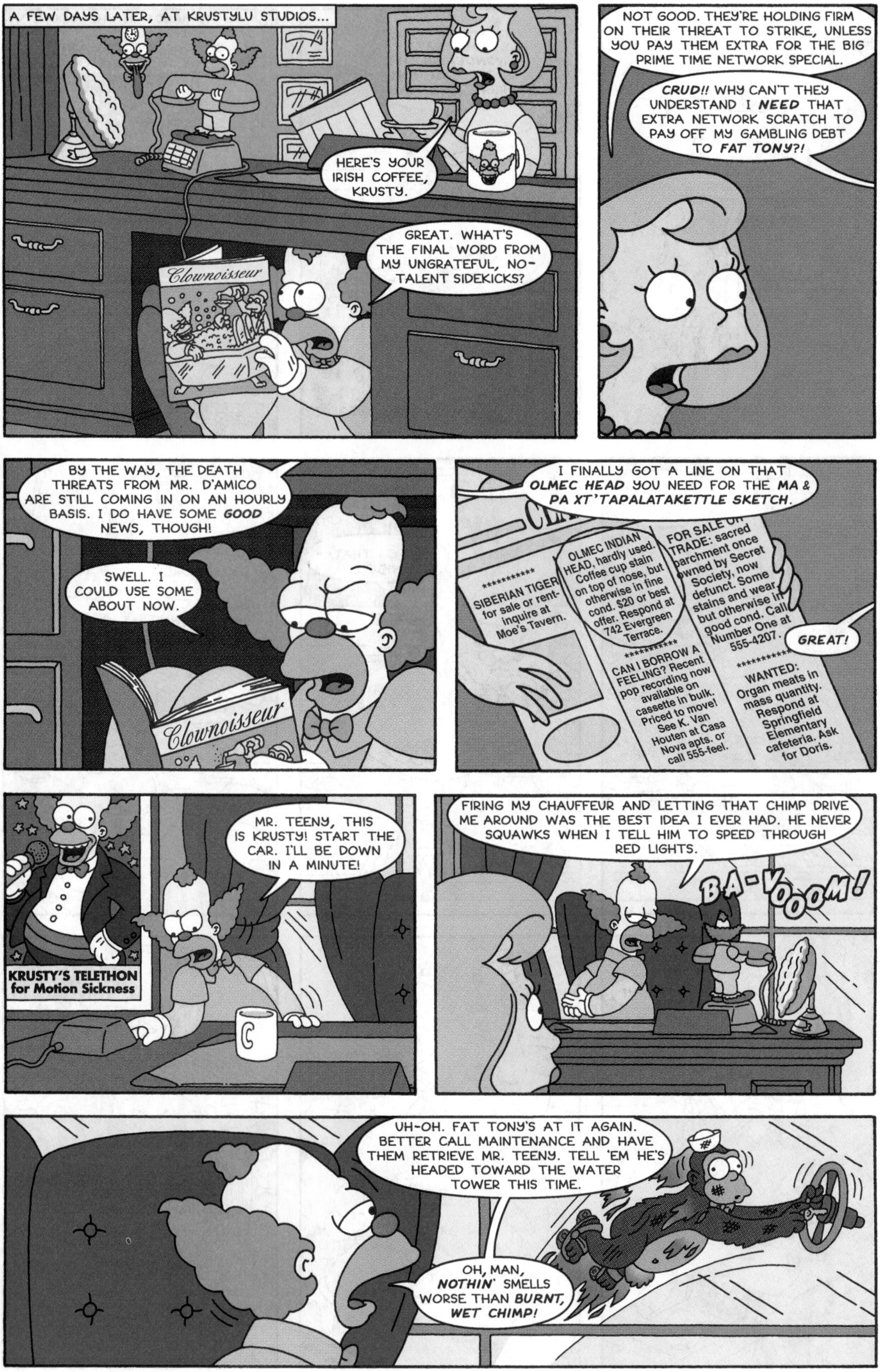
A FEW DAYS LATER, AT KRUSTYLU STUDIOS...
HERE'S YOUR IRISH COFFEE, KRUSTY.
Clownoisseur
GREAT. WHAT'S THE FINAL WORD FROM MY UNGRATEFUL, NO-TALENT SIDEKICKS?
NOT GOOD. THEY'RE HOLDING FIRM ON THEIR THREAT TO STRIKE, UNLESS YOU PAY THEM EXTRA FOR THE BIG PRIME TIME NETWORK SPECIAL.
CRUD!! WHY CAN'T THEY UNDERSTAND I NEED THAT EXTRA NETWORK SCRATCH TO PAY OFF MY GAMBLING DEBT TO FAT TONY?!
BY THE WAY, THE DEATH THREATS FROM MR. D'AMICO ARE STILL COMING IN ON AN HOURLY BASIS. I DO HAVE SOME GOOD NEWS, THOUGH!
SWELL. I COULD USE SOME ABOUT NOW.
Clownoisseur
I FINALLY GOT A LINE ON THAT OLMEC HEAD YOU NEED FOR THE MA & PA XT'TAPALATAKETTLE SKETCH.
SIBERIAN TIGER for sale or rent-inquire at Moe's Tavern.
OLMEC INDIAN HEAD, hardly used. Coffee cup stain on top of nose, but otherwise in fine cond. $20 or best offer. Respond at 742 Evergreen Terrace.
CAN I BORROW A FEELING? Recent pop recording now available on cassette in bulk. Priced to move! See K. Van Houten at Casa Nova apts. or call 555-feel.
FOR SALE OR TRADE: sacred parchment once owned by Secret Society, now defunct. Some stains and wear, but otherwise in good cond. Call Number One at 555-4207.
WANTED: Organ meats in mass quantity. Respond at Springfield Elementary cafeteria. Ask for Doris.
GREAT!
KRUSTY'S TELETHON for Motion Sickness
MR. TEENY, THIS IS KRUSTY! START THE CAR. I'LL BE DOWN IN A MINUTE!
FIRING MY CHAUFFEUR AND LETTING THAT CHIMP DRIVE ME AROUND WAS THE BEST IDEA I EVER HAD. HE NEVER SQUAWKS WHEN I TELL HIM TO SPEED THROUGH RED LIGHTS.
BA-VOOOOM!
UH-OH. FAT TONY'S AT IT AGAIN. BETTER CALL MAINTENANCE AND HAVE THEM RETRIEVE MR. TEENY. TELL 'EM HE'S HEADED TOWARD THE WATER TOWER THIS TIME.
OH, MAN, NOTHIN' SMELLS WORSE THAN BURNT, WET CHIMP!

SOON...
OH, HELLO KRUSTY. ARE YOU HERE TO SEE BART?
WHO THE HEL--?
UH, NO MRS. SIMPSON, NOT THIS TIME. WE'RE HERE ABOUT THE HEAD.
OH, THAT'S WONDERFUL! IT'S IN THE BASEMENT... RIGHT THIS WAY.
MY HUSBAND'S IN THE MIDDLE OF CLEANING, SO THERE'S A LOT OF JUNK LYING AROUND. WATCH YOUR STEP!
GREASE
OKAY, HERE GOES...OOH... AAH...
...WATCH THAT-- WHUP...
...ONE MORE... MADE IT!
HERE I COME, KRUSTY!
OOOOH!
TRIP!
PENNYCANDY, WATCH OU--!
KRA-BASH!
GAAAH!
BROKEN USELESS JUNK FOR SALVATION ARMY DONATION (MOSTLY JAGGED METAL STUFF)

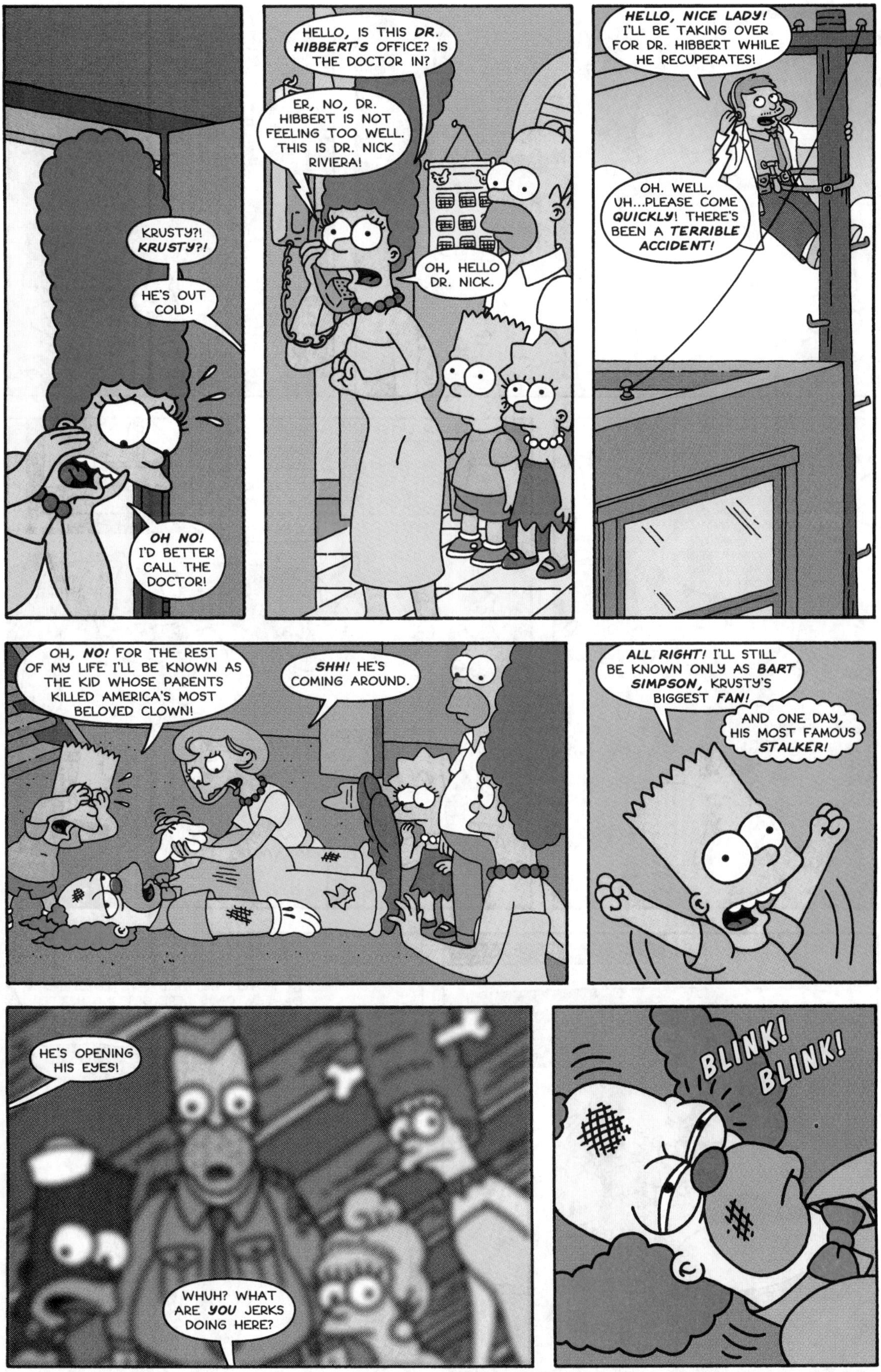

KRUSTY?! KRUSTY?!
HE'S OUT COLD!
OH NO! I'D BETTER CALL THE DOCTOR!
HELLO, IS THIS DR. HIBBERT'S OFFICE? IS THE DOCTOR IN?
ER, NO, DR. HIBBERT IS NOT FEELING TOO WELL. THIS IS DR. NICK RIVIERA!
OH, HELLO DR. NICK.
HELLO, NICE LADY! I'LL BE TAKING OVER FOR DR. HIBBERT WHILE HE RECUPERATES!
OH. WELL, UH...PLEASE COME QUICKLY! THERE'S BEEN A TERRIBLE ACCIDENT!
OH, NO! FOR THE REST OF MY LIFE I'LL BE KNOWN AS THE KID WHOSE PARENTS KILLED AMERICA'S MOST BELOVED CLOWN!
SHH! HE'S COMING AROUND.
ALL RIGHT! I'LL STILL BE KNOWN ONLY AS BART SIMPSON, KRUSTY'S BIGGEST FAN!
AND ONE DAY, HIS MOST FAMOUS STALKER!
HE'S OPENING HIS EYES!
WHUH? WHAT ARE YOU JERKS DOING HERE?
BLINK! BLINK!

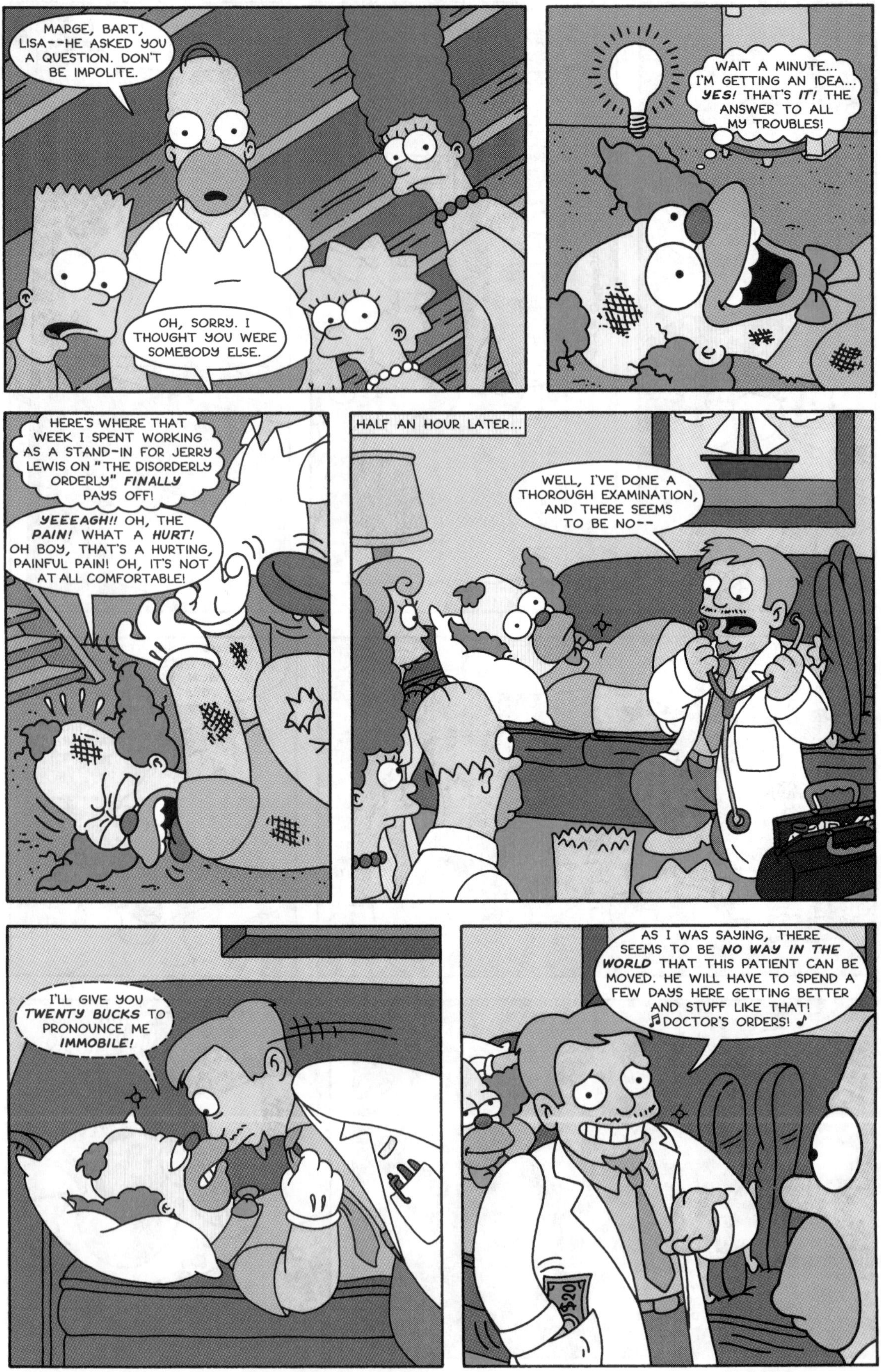
MARGE, BART, LISA--HE ASKED YOU A QUESTION. DON'T BE IMPOLITE.
OH, SORRY. I THOUGHT YOU WERE SOMEBODY ELSE.
WAIT A MINUTE... I'M GETTING AN IDEA... YES! THAT'S IT! THE ANSWER TO ALL MY TROUBLES!
HERE'S WHERE THAT WEEK I SPENT WORKING AS A STAND-IN FOR JERRY LEWIS ON "THE DISORDERLY ORDERLY" FINALLY PAYS OFF!
YEEEAGH!! OH, THE PAIN! WHAT A HURT! OH BOY, THAT'S A HURTING, PAINFUL PAIN! OH, IT'S NOT AT ALL COMFORTABLE!
HALF AN HOUR LATER...
WELL, I'VE DONE A THOROUGH EXAMINATION, AND THERE SEEMS TO BE NO--
I'LL GIVE YOU TWENTY BUCKS TO PRONOUNCE ME IMMOBILE!
AS I WAS SAYING, THERE SEEMS TO BE NO WAY IN THE WORLD THAT THIS PATIENT CAN BE MOVED. HE WILL HAVE TO SPEND A FEW DAYS HERE GETTING BETTER AND STUFF LIKE THAT! ♫DOCTOR'S ORDERS! ♪
$20

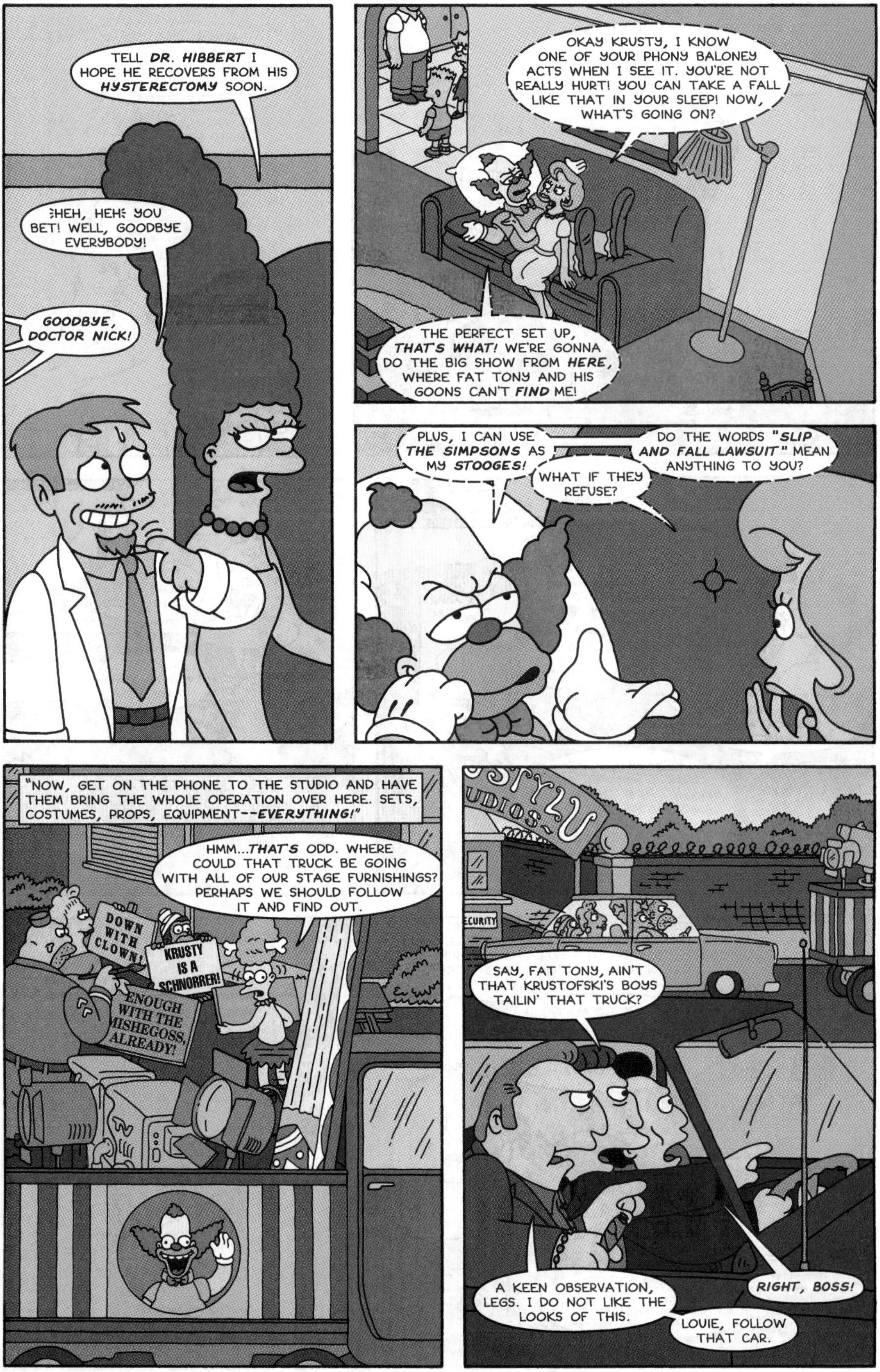

TELL *DR. HIBBERT* I HOPE HE RECOVERS FROM HIS *HYSTERECTOMY* SOON.
HEH, HEH! YOU BET! WELL, GOODBYE EVERYBODY!
GOODBYE, DOCTOR NICK!
OKAY KRUSTY, I KNOW ONE OF YOUR PHONY BALONEY ACTS WHEN I SEE IT. YOU'RE NOT REALLY HURT! YOU CAN TAKE A FALL LIKE THAT IN YOUR SLEEP! NOW, WHAT'S GOING ON?
THE PERFECT SET UP, *THAT'S WHAT!* WE'RE GONNA DO THE BIG SHOW FROM *HERE*, WHERE FAT TONY AND HIS GOONS CAN'T *FIND* ME!
PLUS, I CAN USE *THE SIMPSONS* AS MY *STOOGES!*
WHAT IF THEY REFUSE?
DO THE WORDS *"SLIP AND FALL LAWSUIT"* MEAN ANYTHING TO YOU?
"NOW, GET ON THE PHONE TO THE STUDIO AND HAVE THEM BRING THE WHOLE OPERATION OVER HERE. SETS, COSTUMES, PROPS, EQUIPMENT--*EVERYTHING!*"
HMM...*THAT'S* ODD. WHERE COULD THAT TRUCK BE GOING WITH ALL OF OUR STAGE FURNISHINGS? PERHAPS WE SHOULD FOLLOW IT AND FIND OUT.
DOWN WITH CLOWN!
KRUSTY IS A SCHNORRER!
ENOUGH WITH THE MISHEGOSS, ALREADY!
SAY, FAT TONY, AIN'T THAT KRUSTOFSKI'S BOYS TAILIN' THAT TRUCK?
A KEEN OBSERVATION, LEGS. I DO NOT LIKE THE LOOKS OF THIS.
LOUIE, FOLLOW THAT CAR.
RIGHT, BOSS!

WELL, IT LOOKS LIKE I'M STUCK HERE FOR THE DURATION! HEY KID, LET'S SEE WHAT'S ON THE TUBE WHILE THE MOM-STER FIXES ME SOMETHING TO EAT.
A REUBEN SANDWICH WOULD BE GREAT. SLICE THE CORNED BEEF EXTRA THIN BUT LEAVE THE FAT. AND MAKE SURE YOU USE BROWN MUSTARD!
YOU HEARD THE MAN, MOM-STER! CHOP, CHOP!
DING DONG!
HRRRRM. LISA, SEE IF YOU CAN FIND OUR "GUEST" SOMETHING TO SNACK ON WHILE I ANSWER THE DOOR.
OKAY, MOM-STER!
NOW, CUT THAT OUT!
HEY, YOUR SHOW IS ON! THIS MUST BE A RE-RUN.
YEAH, WE'RE RUNNIN' "BEST OF" PROGRAMS ALL WEEK. THIS ONE'S A CLIP SHOW OF ALL MY COMMERCIAL ENDORSEMENTS.
LET'S SEE WHAT'S ON CABLE.
WE NOW RETURN TO "THE CREME DE LE KRUSTY!"
HEY-HEY, KIDS! GRAB A HAMMER AND SMASH OPEN THOSE PIGGY BANKS, CAUSE I'VE GOT AN OFFER FOR KRUSTY MERCHANDISE YOU JUST CAN'T LIVE WITHOUT!
SORRY, NO CAN DO. WE DON'T HAVE CABLE.
NO CABLE? YOU GOTTA BE KIDDIN' ME!
I KNOW, I KNOW. IT'S A LONG STORY.
HOW LONG?
ABOUT TWENTY TWO MINUTES.
KRUSTY, THERE ARE SOME TEAMSTERS AT THE DOOR WITH A TRUCKLOAD OF TELEVISION EQUIPMENT! THEY SAY IT'S FOR THE BIG PRIME TIME NETWORK SPECIAL THEY'RE TAPING HERE! I TOLD THEM THEY MUST BE MISTAKEN!
OH, IT'S NO MISTAKE! DIDN'T I TELL YOU? SINCE I CAN'T BE MOVED, I HAVE TO BROADCAST MY SPECIAL LIVE FROM YOUR LIVING ROOM!
COOL!
YOU'LL BE SURE TO THROW A SCREAMING TEMPER TANTRUM IF YOU'RE NOT THE FIRST KID ON YOUR BLOCK TO OWN A GENUINE KRUSTY THE CLOWN ELECTRIC CATTLE PROD!
WHAT?!!
AND THERE'S MORE! YOU AND YOUR FAMILY WILL BE STANDING IN FOR MY USUAL CAST OF IDIOTS!

DING DONG!
OH, NOW WHAT?!
YES, MAY I HELP YOU?
PACKAGE FOR HERSCHEL KRUSTOFSKI. SIGN HERE, MA'AM.
TV
KRUSTY
HE'S GOING TO DO THE SHOW FROM HERE? ARE YOU QUITE SURE?
YEAH, LIKE I TOLD THE FAT MOB GUY, I'M SURE, I'M SURE!
HMMM... I CERTAINLY HOPE THIS IS NOTHING ILLEGAL.
OH, DON'T WORRY LADY. IT'S DOLPHIN SAFE.
I WONDER WHAT HE MEANT BY THAT.
SLAM!

KRUSTY, YOUR USUAL CAST OF IDIOTS HAS GATHERED ON OUR FRONT LAWN WITH PICKET SIGNS!
OH, PERFECT! THEY MUST HAVE FOLLOWED THE CREW.
WHAT'S THIS?
A PACKAGE FOR YOU.
OH NO! NOT THIS!
KRUSTY BRAND
CHUNK STYLE TUNA
FAMILY SIZE
PACKED IN NATURAL TAP WATER
Dolphin Safe
OOOH, I'M A DEAD MAN!
WHAT ARE YOU TALKING ABOUT? I SERVE THAT BRAND OF TUNA TO MY FAMILY ALL THE TIME. IT'S NOT THAT BAD. BESIDES, YOU DON'T HAVE TO EAT IT.
NO, IT'S NOT FOR ME TO EAT! THIS IS A MESSAGE FROM FAT TONY! IT MEANS THAT IF I DON'T PAY HIM THE MONEY I OWE HIM, I'LL BE SLEEPIN' WITH THE FISHES!
AND NOT JUST ME--NOTICE, THE CAN SAYS FAMILY SIZE! OBVIOUSLY TONY KNOWS I'M HOLED UP HERE, AND HE'S WILLING TO KILL YOU TO TAKE ME OUT!
GASP!
OH, DEAR!
SO LET ME SEE IF I HAVE THIS STRAIGHT. YOU WON'T BE EATING THE TUNA?
YOINK!
IF ANYONE NEEDS ME, I'LL BE IN THE KITCHEN!
OY VEY!

OH, KRUSTY! WHAT ARE YOU GOING TO DO?
WHAT ELSE CAN I DO? THE SHOW MUST GO ON! IT'S THE ONLY WAY TO GET FAT TONY OFF MY HAIRY YELLOW BACK!
NOW WAIT A MINUTE! LETTING YOU TAKE OVER MY HOUSE IS ONE THING, BUT IF YOU THINK I'M GOING TO LET YOU PUT MY FAMILY IN DANGER, THEN THINK AGAIN!
WELL GUESS WHAT, LADY? YOU DON'T HAVE A CHOICE.
EITHER I DO MY SHOW HERE WITH YOUR FAMILY AS MY STOOGES, PUFF, PUFF OR MY LAWYERS WILL BE IN TOUCH WITH YOU PUFF ABOUT THE PAIN AND INJURY YOUR NEGLIGENCE HAS CAUSED ME.
COUGH
COUGH
COUGH
COUGH
COUGH
SORRY, PENNYCANDY. I WANTED TO BLOW THAT SMOKE IN MRS. SIMPSON'S FACE FOR DRAMATIC EFFECT, BUT IT JUST HURTS TOO MUCH TO TURN MY HEAD.
YOU'RE TURNING YOUR HEAD RIGHT NOW.
SO I AM...OH WELL, THE THREAT STILL STANDS.
ANY MORE OBJECTIONS?
HRRRRRM...
GOOD! FROM NOW ON, NOBODY LEAVES THIS HOUSE! WE'VE GOT A LOT OF WORK TO DO, SO LET'S GET MOVIN'! CREW GUYS, I WANT THIS ROOM LOOKING AND SMELLING LIKE A CIRCUS!
MISS PENNYCANDY, GIVE THE SIMPSONS SOME SCRIPTS. WE START REHEARSING IN TWENTY MINUTES! AND CALL MY LOUSY WRITERS AND TELL THEM I WANT THAT FINAL DRAFT FOR THE TITANIC TRIBUTE, AND IT'D BETTER BE FUNNY!

"C'MON PEOPLE, BREAK A SWEAT! WE'VE GOTTA HAVE SOMETHING WE CAN PUT ON THE AIR BY TOMORROW NIGHT!"
KRUSTY'S Prime Time Circus of Ratings
...AND I WANT TO THANK EVERYBODY FROM THE BOTTOM OF MY PACEMAKER! HOO, HOO, HEY! YOU ALL DID A LOT OF HARD WORK, EVEN THOUGH NOBODY GOT TO SEE IT!
WE'RE LIVE IN FIVE, KRUSTY!
CONGRATULATIONS, MARGE. THE SIMPSONS ARE ABOUT TO BECOME A PART OF TELEVISION HISTORY.
I JUST CAN'T WAIT FOR THIS NIGHTMARE TO BE OVER!
UM, YOUR BONE'S A LITTLE CROOKED.

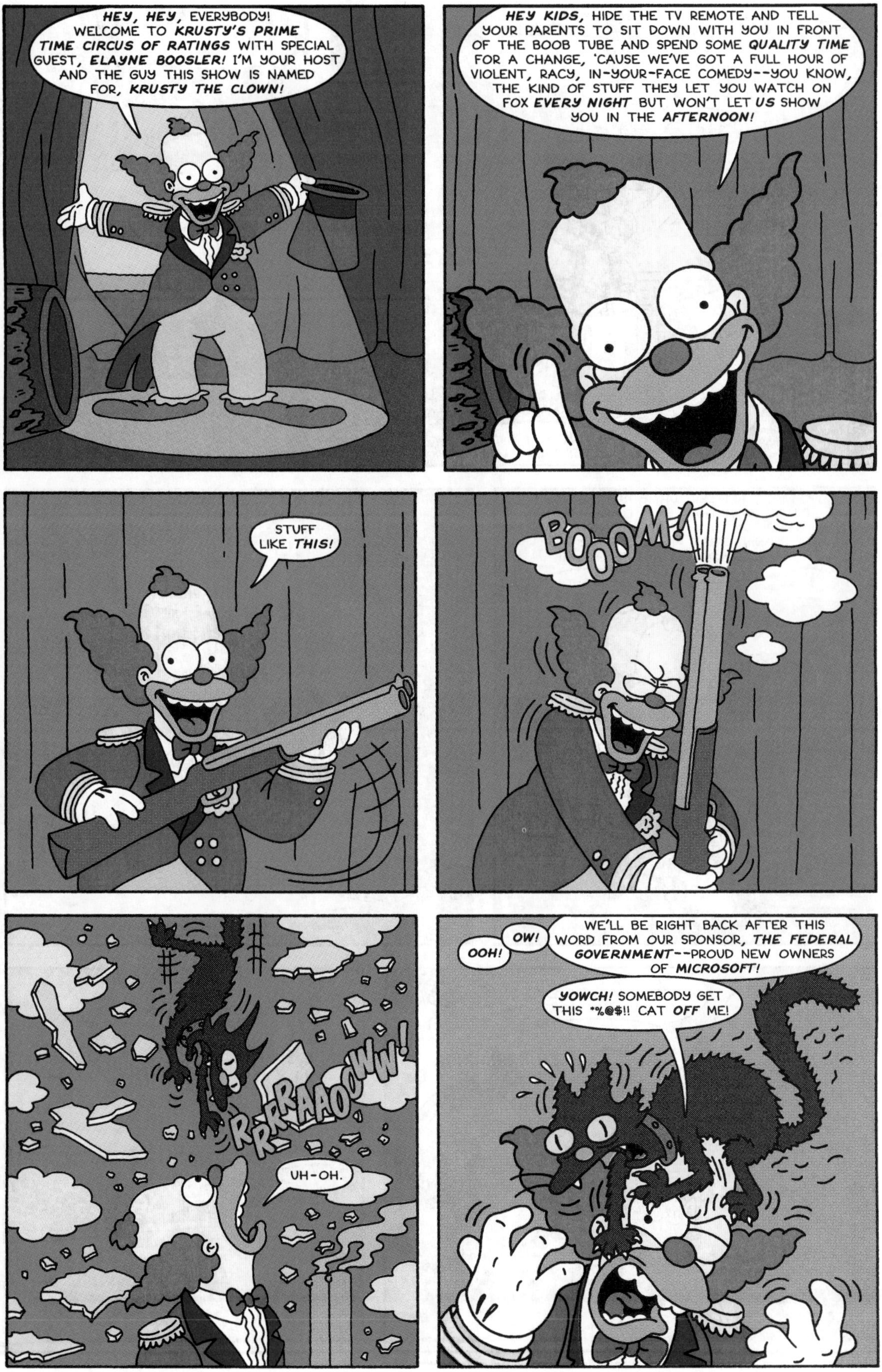
HEY, HEY, EVERYBODY! WELCOME TO KRUSTY'S PRIME TIME CIRCUS OF RATINGS WITH SPECIAL GUEST, ELAYNE BOOSLER! I'M YOUR HOST AND THE GUY THIS SHOW IS NAMED FOR, KRUSTY THE CLOWN!
HEY KIDS, HIDE THE TV REMOTE AND TELL YOUR PARENTS TO SIT DOWN WITH YOU IN FRONT OF THE BOOB TUBE AND SPEND SOME QUALITY TIME FOR A CHANGE, 'CAUSE WE'VE GOT A FULL HOUR OF VIOLENT, RACY, IN-YOUR-FACE COMEDY--YOU KNOW, THE KIND OF STUFF THEY LET YOU WATCH ON FOX EVERY NIGHT BUT WON'T LET US SHOW YOU IN THE AFTERNOON!
STUFF LIKE THIS!
BOOOM!
RRRAAOOWW!
UH-OH.
OOH!
OW!
WE'LL BE RIGHT BACK AFTER THIS WORD FROM OUR SPONSOR, THE FEDERAL GOVERNMENT--PROUD NEW OWNERS OF MICROSOFT!
YOWCH! SOMEBODY GET THIS *%@$!! CAT OFF ME!

SHORTLY...
PLACES EVERYBODY! WE'RE COMING OUT OF COMMERCIAL!
HOLD ON! CORPORAL PUNISHMENT'S MISSING!
KRUSTY, I CAN'T HOLD! WE'RE LIVE...
...IN THREE...TWO... ONE...YOU'RE ON!
AW, CRUD!
HEH, HEH...ER, UH...BOY, I SURE WISH THAT FAT, LOUD-MOUTHED BUM OF A SERGEANT WAS HERE PLAYING THAT PIANO OFF-KEY, SO I COULD TELL HIM TO CUT IT OUT.
OH MAN, IT'S GONNA BE A LONG SKETCH.
HI, KRUSTY. NICE SHIRT. WANT A BEER?
HOMER, YOU BRAINDEAD IDIOT! WE'RE IN THE MIDDLE OF YOUR SKETCH!
UH, HEY THERE, SARGE! WHAT HAPPENED TO YOUR UNIFORM?
HUH? WHAT ARE YOU TALKING ABOU-- OH, RIGHT! THE TV SHOW!
CRASH!
SSSSSSSSSSSS

YEEEEHH!
WAH! FAT TONY AGAIN! DO SOMETHING, QUICK!
NO, NO, THAT'LL NEVER HOLD IT! IT NEEDS SOMETHING HEAVY!
OH, THIS WON'T BE PRETTY. BUT I GOTTA ADMIT, IT'S ALREADY BETTER THAN THAT SKETCH WAS EVER GONNA BE.
BA-VOOOM!
YOWCH! OOH, MY HEAD! OW--
HEY, THAT DYNAMITE DIDN'T BLOW MY UNDERWEAR OFF, DID IT?
HELLO?... KRUSTY...
...CAN WE GO TO COMMERCIAL?
GREAT IDEA, CORPORAL PUNISHMENT! WE'LL BE RIGHT BACK AFTER THIS IMPORTANT MESSAGE FROM KRUSTY BRAND BITE-A-MIN'S IMITATION VITAMINS.

AND SO IT GOES, SKIT BY SKIT...
LAWSUIT
SSSSSS
KA-BOOOM!
HO HO HOO HEY!
...BIT BY BIT...
MOOSH!
SPLOOSH!
GLUB!
VWOOOSH!
CLOWN AIR

UNTIL...
OKAY EVERYBODY, TAKE FIVE WHILE I PERFORM MY FAMOUS ERNIE KOVACS RIP OFF-- ER, I MEAN TRIBUTE. THEN YOU GO RIGHT INTO THE MA & PA SKETCH WHILE I CHANGE MY COSTUME.
AND TELL THAT FREAKIN' KID TO PUT DOWN MY BALL! IT'S NOT A TOY!
BOY, KRUSTY SURE HAS MADE A QUICK RECOVERY.
IT'S ABOUT TIME SOMEBODY NOTICED THAT!
MOM, TELL ELAYNE BOOSLER TO QUIT HOGGIN' THE BATHROOM!
I HAVE GRAVE MISGIVINGS ABOUT DOING THIS NEXT SKETCH, MOM. SOMEHOW I DON'T THINK THE OLMEC INDIAN GOD OF WAR WOULD APPRECIATE BEING PORTRAYED AS A HILLBILLY'S OUTHOUSE.
I HAVEN'T HEARD HIM COMPLAIN ABOUT THE FACT THAT MOM'S BEEN BEATING OUR CLOTHES AGAINST HIM.
WELL, HE WORKS REALLY WELL ON STUBBORN STAINS!
I REALLY DON'T WANT TO DO THIS, MOM. PLEASE DON'T MAKE ME GO OUT THERE!
YEAH, ME TOO MOM! I'VE HAD IT UP TO HERE WITH THIS FARSHTINKENER SHOW!
THE BOY'S RIGHT! IT IS FARSHTINKENER!
I KNOW YOU'RE ALL UPSET. I AM TOO, BUT WE HAVE TO SEE THIS THROUGH TO THE END. WE CAN'T AFFORD A BIG LAWSUIT.
MAYBE I CAN HELP. I THINK KRUSTY NEEDS TO LEARN THAT HE CAN'T JUST USE OTHER PEOPLE TO AVOID PAYING FOR HIS OWN MISTAKES.
BUT HOW?
KRUSTY'S SIDEKICKS ARE STILL PICKETING OUT ON YOUR FRONT LAWN. I JUST BET THEY MIGHT BE WILLING TO HELP US. GO AHEAD AND START THE SKETCH, BUT BE PREPARED TO BAIL OUT.

SOON...
SAY PA, IS THET A NEW CORNCOB PIPE YO GOT THERE?
YOU CALL IT CORNCOB, BUT I CALL IT A MAIZECOB PIPE!
HO, HA! HA, HA!
HEH, HEH!
WAH, HA HA!
TEE HEE!
OOK, OOK!
MAN, THAT LAUGH TRACK SOUNDS SO LIFE-LIKE-- HEY, WAIT A MINUTE!
WHAT'RE YOU INGRATES DOIN' HERE? GET OFF THE SET!
WE ARE HEREBY COMMANDEERING THIS COMEDY/VARIETY SPECIAL! SIMPSON FAMILY, YOUR CONSIDERABLE TALENTS ARE NO LONGER REQUIRED! YOU ARE FREE TO GO!
I HOPE YOU KNOW WHAT YOU'RE DOING.
PUT ME DOWN, YOU BIG NEANDERTHAL!
WOO HOO!
WHEEEE!
BRING FORTH...THE CANNON!
ALL RIGHT!
HEY! OOF! WHAT'RE YOU-- URK!?
WHUMPH!

WE'VE WAITED A LONG TIME FOR THIS, KRUSTY! MR. TEENY, THE CREAM PIE IF YOU WILL!
YOU'RE GONNA REGRET THIS!
SHPLATT!
GLUB!
SHPLOOSH!
YOU GUYS'LL NEVER WORK UNDER THE BIG TOP AGAIN! COSMO, GO TO COMMERCIAL!
KA-BOOOOOM!
FA-WOP!

NOW THIS IS QUALITY PROGRAMMING! YOU GUYS DIDN'T REALLY WANNA FINISH WATCHIN' THAT LINGERIE FASHION SHOW ON E! DID YA?
NO, NO, WE'RE GOOD WITH THIS!
YEAH, KEEP THIS ON!
SHHHHHH! I CAN'T HEAR THE BOOM!
AW, C'MON GUYS, NOT AGAIN!
TWO TIMES OUT OF THE CANNON IN A ROW! IT'S PURE GENIUS! WHY DIDN'T I EVER THINK OF THAT!
MOTEL
IF YOU HAD, MAYBE WE'D HAVE A PRIME TIME SPECIAL INSTEAD O' WHAT WE GOT, WHICH IS BUPKISS!
I MUST SAY, MY EX-EMPLOYER HAS NEVER BEEN FUNNIER!
AND THAT SIDESHOW MEL IS DOING A MARVELOUS JOB OF FILLING YOUR SKIRT. HIS COMIC TIMING HAS THE PRECISION OF A FINE SWISS TIMEPIECE! IMPECCAB--
NO! NO! KEEP THAT CAT AWAY FROM ME! YAAAAAAAAH!
HO HA
HA HA
HEE HEE
WHAT'D I TELL YOU TWO SILLY MARYS ABOUT THE FANCY TALK?
HA, HA!
HEY! THEY'RE STEALIN' MY MATERIAL!
YEAH, BUT IT'S FUNNIER ON TV.
SHALL I GIVE THE COMMAND FOR THE ARMADA TO BEGIN THE DESTRUCTION OF EARTH?
HAVE YOU LOST YOUR COGNITIVE ABILITY? THE EARTHLINGS HAVE FINALLY DEVELOPED SOMETHING WORTHY OF OUR RESPECT! WE MUST RETURN TO RIGEL 4 AND FIND A WAY TO DUPLICATE THIS AMAZING ENTERTAINMENT!
MISS KENDALL, CALL KRUSTY'S CELL PHONE AND PATCH ME THROUGH!
PAT
PAT
PAT

WHAT THE--?
BRRRRIIIING!
HELLO, KRUSTY HERE... UH, HUH...OKAY.
IT'S THE NETWORK PRESIDENT. HE WANTS TO TALK TO YOU.
THIS IS MEL...YES... THEY DID? ...WE WILL? ...YES! THANK YOU SIR, I'LL TELL THEM!
WONDERFUL NEWS, EVERYBODY! THE SHOW'S RATINGS WENT THROUGH THE ROOF! THE NETWORK IS GIVING US ALL BIG BONUS CHECKS!
YOU CAN HAVE KRUSTY'S CHECK SENT TO HIM AT THE LEGITIMATE BUSINESSMEN'S CLUB, WHERE HE WILL BE WASHING GLASSES AND SCRUBBING TOILETS UNTIL IT CLEARS.
OY, GEVALT!
WELL HOMER, YOU'D BETTER FINISH CLEANING OUT THE BASEMENT WHILE I CALL THE NEWSPAPER AND PLACE ANOTHER AD TO SELL THE HEAD.
OH NO, I'VE LEARNED MY LESSON. THERE ARE SOME THINGS MORE IMPORTANT THAN HAVING A REC ROOM IN YOUR BASEMENT. THE HEAD STAYS!
NOW I SUGGEST YOU ALL FOLLOW MY EXAMPLE. I'M GOING TO MAKE PEACE WITH OUR GOD OF WAR, AND THEN I'M GOING TO BREAK INTO FLANDERS' HOUSE AND SHOOT SOME POOL.
THE END

The Incredible Edible Exploits of
LARD LAD
$14.95
FREE with purchase of $15 worth of donuts
COMICS -- PUZZLES -- FILLERS -- THINLY DISGUISED ADVERTISING
IN SEARCH OF THE LOST DONUT HOLES!
NOW WHERE HAS DOC DEEPFRY'S COSMIC DONUT HOLE TAKEN US, LARD LAD?
I HAVE ABSOLUTELY NO IDEA, CUPCAKE...
...BUT IT LOOKS AND SMELLS DELICIOUS!!!
AAAIIIEEEEEEEE!!!
GROENING SHAW! Steere
DON'T LOOK AT ME, KIDS, I'M JUST THE LOVABLE COMIC RELIEF!
NOTE TO PARENTS: CONTAINS EDUCATIONAL MATERIAL!!!

EAT LARD LAD DONUTS: 50,000 POLICEMEN CAN'T BE WRONG!

GET A WELL-ROUNDED LIFE! EAT LARD LAD DONUTS!

LARD LAD DONUTS ARE LARDIER DONUTS!

GO NUTS WITH DONUTS -- LARD LAD DONUTS, THAT IS!

PING PONG SET

Comes complete with one paddle, one ball, and official rule book. All you need is another paddle, net, and table for hours of ping pong fun.

"SWISHER JET"
Ready-to-fly jet aeroplane!

Nothing to build. Just attach wings, light fuse, and away it goes. Flies at least 9 ft. Works only once!

INCREDIBLE PROFESSIONAL GUITAR

Miniature. Shiny. Beautiful tone. Not a ukulele. Plays "Turkey in the Straw." All you do is turn the little crank.

SCIENTIFIC CHEMISTRY SET

Complete with several chemicals, including salt, sugar and H2O. Comes with science napkin, science spoon, and science cup.

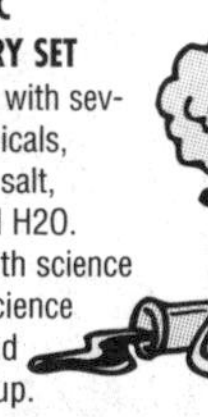

REALISTIC WRIST WATCH

For boys and girls. Needs no winding. Handsome. Just like grown-ups wear. Pretend to tell time. Hands seem to move if you jiggle watch really hard.

I'M "UNCLE" KRUSTY

I WILL SEND YOU PRIZES LIKE THESE*

***Not these prizes, exactly, but prizes somewhat like these**

Official Size Official Weight
PROFESSIONAL BASKETBALL

Well, not really. Actually, an orange-colored gumball, approx. 1/4 in. in diameter. Tasty.

Hiya, kids! I have been helping boys and girls just like you get prizes for 17 years, except for that brief time I spent in jail when I got framed by Sideshow Bob, and those two other times when I got nabbed for tax evasion. Anyway, where was I? Oh yeah--shown here are just a few of the wonderful prizes you might get for selling my famous Krusty Brand exotic Flower Seed Packs. Just between you and me, these so-called exotic flower seeds are really just annoying milkweed seeds--heh heh--but don't tell the customers that! Believe me, the truth just ain't good for business! So here's where you come in. Any of the prizes on this page can be yours if you just sell 3 cases of 87 boxes of 40 packs of seeds at the low, low price of $1.89 a pack. Many youngsters sell their packs in 1 day and get their prizes before they know it, and that's a "Krusty Promise."*

*Not a real promise.

BOW AND ARROW ARCHERY SET

Includes little bow, really little arrow, and really, really little target. Just like the elves use.

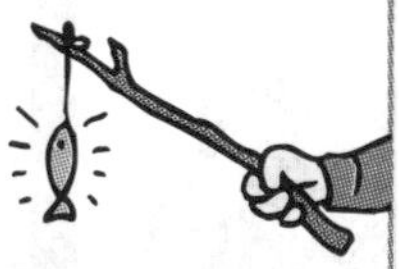

BIG CATCH FISHING OUTFIT

This great outfit includes 3-1/2 ft. hickory stick, string, paper-clip-style hook. Plus bonus dried worm.

HURRY! BE THE 1ST IN YOUR NEIGHBORHOOD

Get in early before the grown-ups find out these so-called flower seeds are nothing but nuisance weeds! Do whatever you gotta do to sell these seed packs! Turn on the charm, threaten, cajole, even throw tantrums. Grandparents are expecially gullible to whining and guilt trips! You'll sell your seed packs quickly to your family, friends, and neighbors! Just send me the cash! Don't forget the cash! Remember: Send me that cash!

FLASH CAMERA

This spiffy outfit takes blurry, out-of-focus "artistic" shots. Wow!! Be the next famous big-time photographer like whatsisname.

HERE IT IS--THE GOLDEN "TRUMPET"

Over 5 inches long. Play bugle calls, hot bebop, Top 40 hits. Works on unique "kazoo" principle. Fool your friends, self.

DINK-E-CRAFT MICROSCOPE OUTFIT

Precision-built. Complete with lens. See crumbs, dots, and specks. Don't miss. Make discoveries.

SEND VERY LITTLE MONEY--I TRUST YOU--AND YOU TRUST ME. RIGHT?

Prize Winner Milhouse Van Houton says: "I sold 3,584 packs of seeds and got a little rubber doggie. It's not the prize I wanted, but Krusty says if I sell a lot more seeds, maybe I'll get something better."

EVER-SO-PRETTY TRAVEL CASE

Overnight case with removable tray. Comes with mirror shard, key. No lock. Stores one pack of gum or two little pink erasers.

ROMANTIC LOCKET SET

Gorgeous necklace with locket that opens if you pry hard enough. Elegant and swell.

RADIO KIT

A genuine radio. Build it. Listen to it. Hear that crackle? That's called static!

JR. BEAVER AXE KIT

All-purpose kit. Looks like plain old hammer in disguise. Just sharpen it till the hammer head wears down to "axe-like" look.

EXTRA! $50 IN GRAND PRIZES

1st PRIZE Mystery Box
2nd PRIZE Surprise Package
3rd PRIZE Leaky Grab Bag

You are eligible to win if you sell at least 1,000 seed packs.

PLUS 20 Official SIDESHOW MEL USED UNICYCLES!

MAIL THIS NOW--*AND I MEAN NOW!*

"Uncle" Krusty the Clown, KRUSTY SEED CO.,
Box B, Dept. RM, SPRINGFIELD USA

Please send me 3 cases of 87 boxes of 40-pack seeds. I will re-sell them and send you all the money and choose my prize. Enclosed is $5 initiation fee, $10 processing fee, $35 deposit, and $7.50 for postage and handling. All seeds delivered C.O.D.

Name______________________________________

Address____________________________________

Town_____________________Zone__________State_______

Offer void after Sept. 15, 1998.

BONGO COMICS GROUP
SIMPSONS™ COMICS
#41
US $2.50
CAN $3.50
APPROVED BY THE COMICS CODE AUTHORITY
presents
"BART SIMPSON & THE KRUSTY BRAND FUN FACTORY"
©1999 BONGO ENTERTAINMENT, INC. THE SIMPSONS ©&TM TWENTIETH CENTURY FOX FILM CORPORATION. ALL RIGHTS RESERVED.
GROENING

ITCHY & SCRATCHY
IN
CHOCO-PUSSY
or
Dip and Let Die!
AAAAAAAAAAAH!
SCRIPT
JESSE LEON MCCANN &
ROBERT L. GRAFF
PENCILS
JAMES LLOYD
INKS
TIM BAVINGTON
LETTERS
JEANNINE BLACK
COLORS
NATHAN KANE
EDITS
BILL MORRISON
THE CANDY MAN
MATT GROENING

SHUK!
POPPIN' ROCKS
YOU'RE ALL WASHED UP, MR. SCRATCHY!
PSSSSST!
YAAAAA!
RUMBLE! RUMBLE!
fzzzz-BOOOOM!!
*
* IN SPACE, NO ONE CAN HEAR YOU SCREAM.
WOW! WHAT A WAY TO GO!
MARGE, WHEN I DIE, WILL YOU MAKE SURE I GET DIPPED IN CHOCOLATE AND SHOT INTO THE SUN?
BWA-HA-HU-HA!
HRRRM...HOMER, I THOUGHT YOU WANTED TO BE DRESSED LIKE ELVIS IN 'BLUE HAWAII' AND DROPPED INTO A VOLCANO.

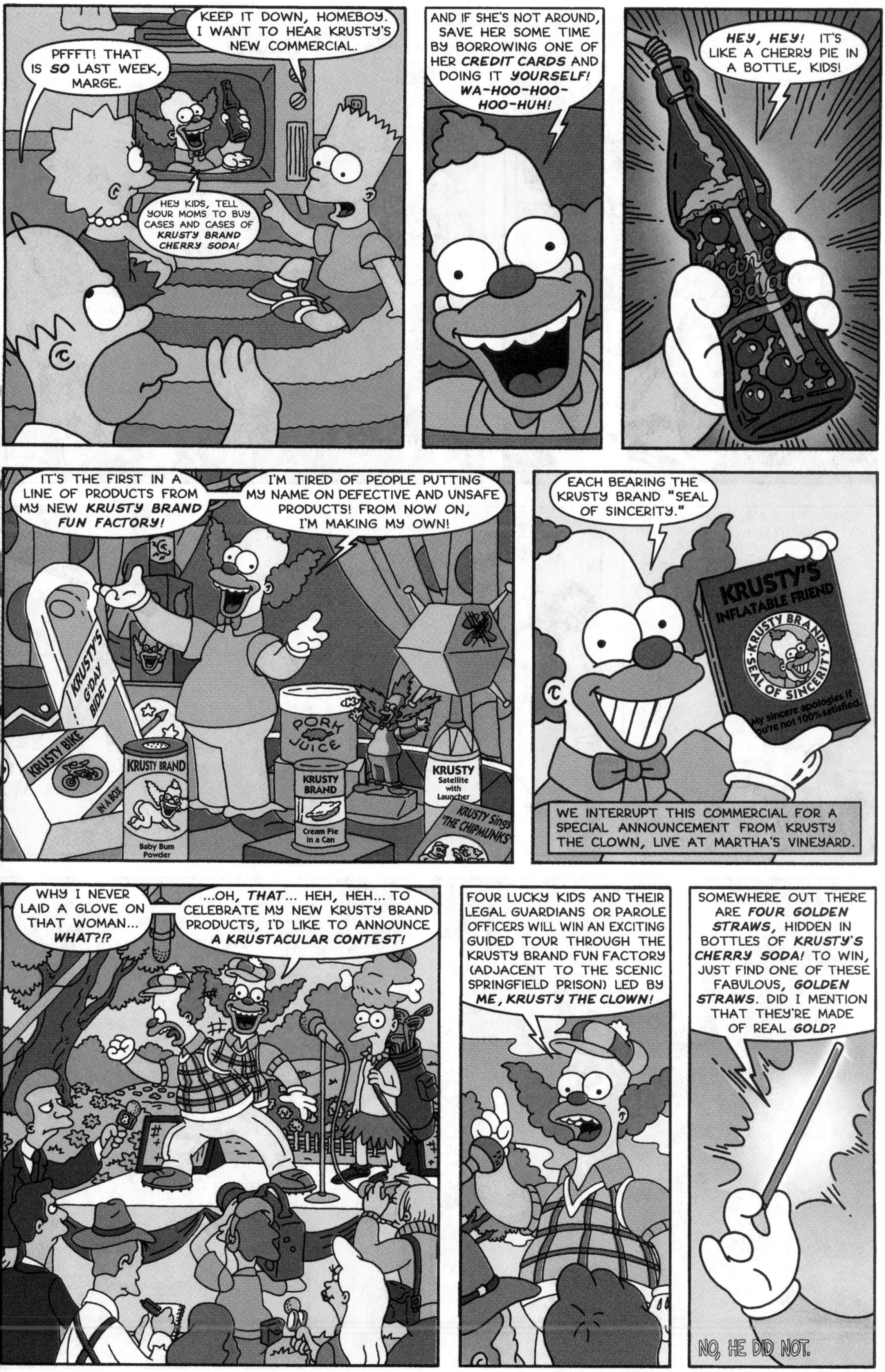
PFFFT! THAT IS **SO** LAST WEEK, MARGE.
KEEP IT DOWN, HOMEBOY. I WANT TO HEAR KRUSTY'S NEW COMMERCIAL.
HEY KIDS, TELL YOUR MOMS TO BUY CASES AND CASES OF ***KRUSTY BRAND CHERRY SODA!***
AND IF SHE'S NOT AROUND, SAVE HER SOME TIME BY BORROWING ONE OF HER ***CREDIT CARDS*** AND DOING IT ***YOURSELF! WA-HOO-HOO-HOO-HUH!***
HEY, HEY! IT'S LIKE A CHERRY PIE IN A BOTTLE, KIDS!
IT'S THE FIRST IN A LINE OF PRODUCTS FROM MY NEW ***KRUSTY BRAND FUN FACTORY!***
I'M TIRED OF PEOPLE PUTTING MY NAME ON DEFECTIVE AND UNSAFE PRODUCTS! FROM NOW ON, I'M MAKING MY OWN!
KRUSTY'S G'DAY BIDET
KRUSTY BIKE IN A BOX
KRUSTY BRAND Baby Bum Powder
PORK JUICE
KRUSTY BRAND Cream Pie in a Can
KRUSTY Satellite with Launcher
KRUSTY Sings "THE CHIPMUNKS"
EACH BEARING THE KRUSTY BRAND "SEAL OF SINCERITY."
KRUSTY'S INFLATABLE FRIEND
KRUSTY BRAND SEAL OF SINCERITY
My sincere apologies if you're not 100% satisfied.
WE INTERRUPT THIS COMMERCIAL FOR A SPECIAL ANNOUNCEMENT FROM KRUSTY THE CLOWN, LIVE AT MARTHA'S VINEYARD.
WHY I NEVER LAID A GLOVE ON THAT WOMAN... ***WHAT?!?***
...OH, ***THAT***... HEH, HEH... TO CELEBRATE MY NEW KRUSTY BRAND PRODUCTS, I'D LIKE TO ANNOUNCE ***A KRUSTACULAR CONTEST!***
FOUR LUCKY KIDS AND THEIR LEGAL GUARDIANS OR PAROLE OFFICERS WILL WIN AN EXCITING GUIDED TOUR THROUGH THE KRUSTY BRAND FUN FACTORY (ADJACENT TO THE SCENIC SPRINGFIELD PRISON) LED BY ***ME, KRUSTY THE CLOWN!***
SOMEWHERE OUT THERE ARE ***FOUR GOLDEN STRAWS,*** HIDDEN IN BOTTLES OF ***KRUSTY'S CHERRY SODA!*** TO WIN, JUST FIND ONE OF THESE FABULOUS, ***GOLDEN STRAWS.*** DID I MENTION THAT THEY'RE MADE OF REAL ***GOLD?***
NO, HE DID NOT.

THIS IS KRUSTY WATCH '99. I'M KENT BROCKMAN, LIVE AT THE SPRINGFIELD MONSTROMART, WHERE RALPH WIGGUM HAS BECOME THE *FIRST* LUCKY OWNER OF A *GOLDEN STRAW!*
HEY, HEY! IT'S LIKE A CHERRY PIE IN A BOTTLE!
SODA
KRUSTY BRAND
SURPRISINGLY, THE YOUNG BOY WAS UNHINDERED BY THE CROWDS.
WE'RE ALMOST DONE HERE. COME ON! GIVE THE BOY SOME ROOM, YOU PEOPLE.
DADDY, MY NOSE SMELLS LIKE COUGH SYRUP!
TAPED EARLIER
LOUSY, STINKING, SELF-SERVING CIVIL SERVANTS! ALWAYS GETTING THE *GOLD MINE* WHILE I GET *THE SHAFT!*
GLUG GLUG GLUG!
GOOD HEAVENS! I'M NO DOCTOR, BUT I THINK YOUR FATHER HAS A BURST APPENDIX! THANK GOODNESS HE WAS NEAR HIS *LOVING FAMILY* WHEN THIS HAPPENED.
QUICK, KIDS, CALL 911!
MMRRROW!
CHOKE!
COUGH!
ACK!
AW, MOM, THERE'S ONLY THREE STRAWS LEFT!
NOW, KIDS, YOU KNOW YOUR FATHER WOULD STAY AND HELP *YOU*...HMMM... WELL, *I* WOULD...

WE'VE GOT A BLEEDER IN HERE!
D'OH!
OH, WAIT. THAT'S CHERRY SODA.
WOO-HOO!
SOON...
IS IT SERIOUS?
WELL, I'M NO DOCTOR, MRS. SIMPSON, BUT I'D SAY YOUR HUSBAND IS SUFFERING FROM AN ACUTE BURST APPENDIX!
IF YOU'RE NOT A DOCTOR, WHY DID YOU JUST EXAMINE MY HUSBAND?!
YOU HAVE NO IDEA HOW LONELY IT CAN GET IN A GIFT BOUTIQUE.
LATER...
OH, DAD, I'M SO GLAD YOUR OPERATION WENT OKAY.
DOES THIS HURT?
OW! CUT IT OUT!
LIVE! KRUSTY WATCH '99
KENT BROCKMAN HERE WITH THE SECOND LUCKY GOLDEN STRAW WINNER, NELSON MUNTZ!
IT WAS A LOT OF WORK SHAKING DOWN THESE DWEEBS AND STUFF, BUT IT FINALLY PAID OFF.
OKAY, S-SO WE'RE FRIENDS NOW, RIGHT?
WHATEVER.
NELSON MUNTZ, LOCAL BULLY
OH, MAN. ONLY TWO LEFT. MY CHANCES ARE DROPPING FASTER THAN MARTIN PRINCE IN A DODGEBALL GAME.
WELL NOW, HOW'S MY PATIENT DOING? I THOUGHT YOU'D LIKE TO SEE WHAT WE CUT OUT OF YOUR ENGORGED ABDOMINAL CAVITY.
EWWWW, NO!
COOL, MAN. LET ME HAVE IT.
AH, HEH! HEH! HEH!
THAT WOULD BE AGAINST HOSPITAL POLICY AND EVERY ETHICAL PRINCIPLE A MAN OF MY MEDICAL BACKGROUND BELIEVES IN...
...BUT OKAY, JUST THIS ONCE.

Taa-raa-taa-rah!
Taa-raa-taa-rah!
AYE, CARUMBA!! IT'S A GOLDEN STRAW!
D'OH!
Taa-raa taa-rah!

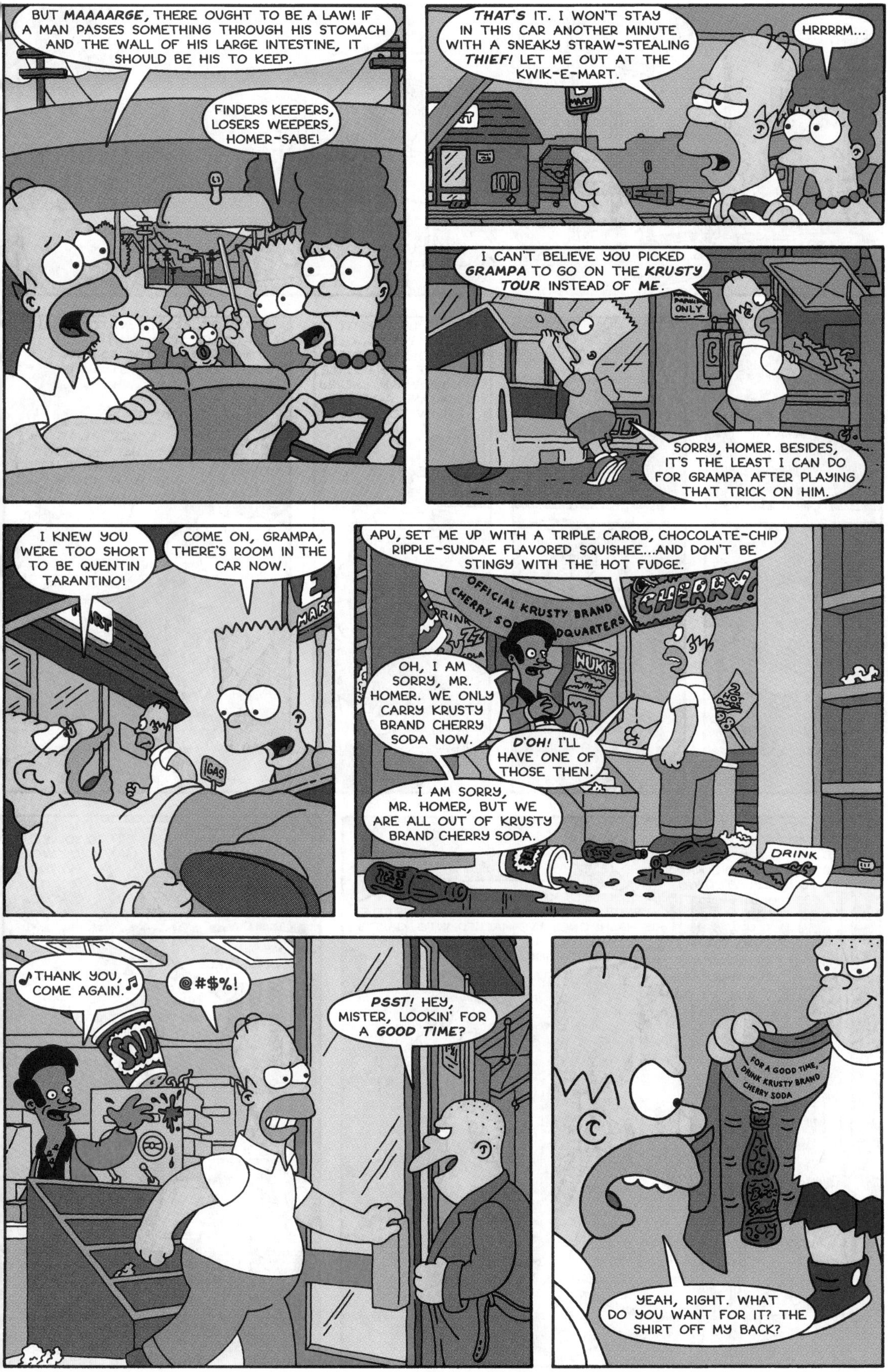

BUT MAAAARGE, THERE OUGHT TO BE A LAW! IF A MAN PASSES SOMETHING THROUGH HIS STOMACH AND THE WALL OF HIS LARGE INTESTINE, IT SHOULD BE HIS TO KEEP.
FINDERS KEEPERS, LOSERS WEEPERS, HOMER-SABE!
THAT'S IT. I WON'T STAY IN THIS CAR ANOTHER MINUTE WITH A SNEAKY STRAW-STEALING THIEF! LET ME OUT AT THE KWIK-E-MART.
HRRRRM...
I CAN'T BELIEVE YOU PICKED GRAMPA TO GO ON THE KRUSTY TOUR INSTEAD OF ME.
SORRY, HOMER. BESIDES, IT'S THE LEAST I CAN DO FOR GRAMPA AFTER PLAYING THAT TRICK ON HIM.
I KNEW YOU WERE TOO SHORT TO BE QUENTIN TARANTINO!
COME ON, GRAMPA, THERE'S ROOM IN THE CAR NOW.
APU, SET ME UP WITH A TRIPLE CAROB, CHOCOLATE-CHIP RIPPLE-SUNDAE FLAVORED SQUISHEE...AND DON'T BE STINGY WITH THE HOT FUDGE.
OFFICIAL KRUSTY BRAND CHERRY SODA HEADQUARTERS
OH, I AM SORRY, MR. HOMER. WE ONLY CARRY KRUSTY BRAND CHERRY SODA NOW.
D'OH! I'LL HAVE ONE OF THOSE THEN.
I AM SORRY, MR. HOMER, BUT WE ARE ALL OUT OF KRUSTY BRAND CHERRY SODA.
DRINK
♪THANK YOU, COME AGAIN.♫
@#$%!
PSST! HEY, MISTER, LOOKIN' FOR A GOOD TIME?
FOR A GOOD TIME, DRINK KRUSTY BRAND CHERRY SODA
YEAH, RIGHT. WHAT DO YOU WANT FOR IT? THE SHIRT OFF MY BACK?

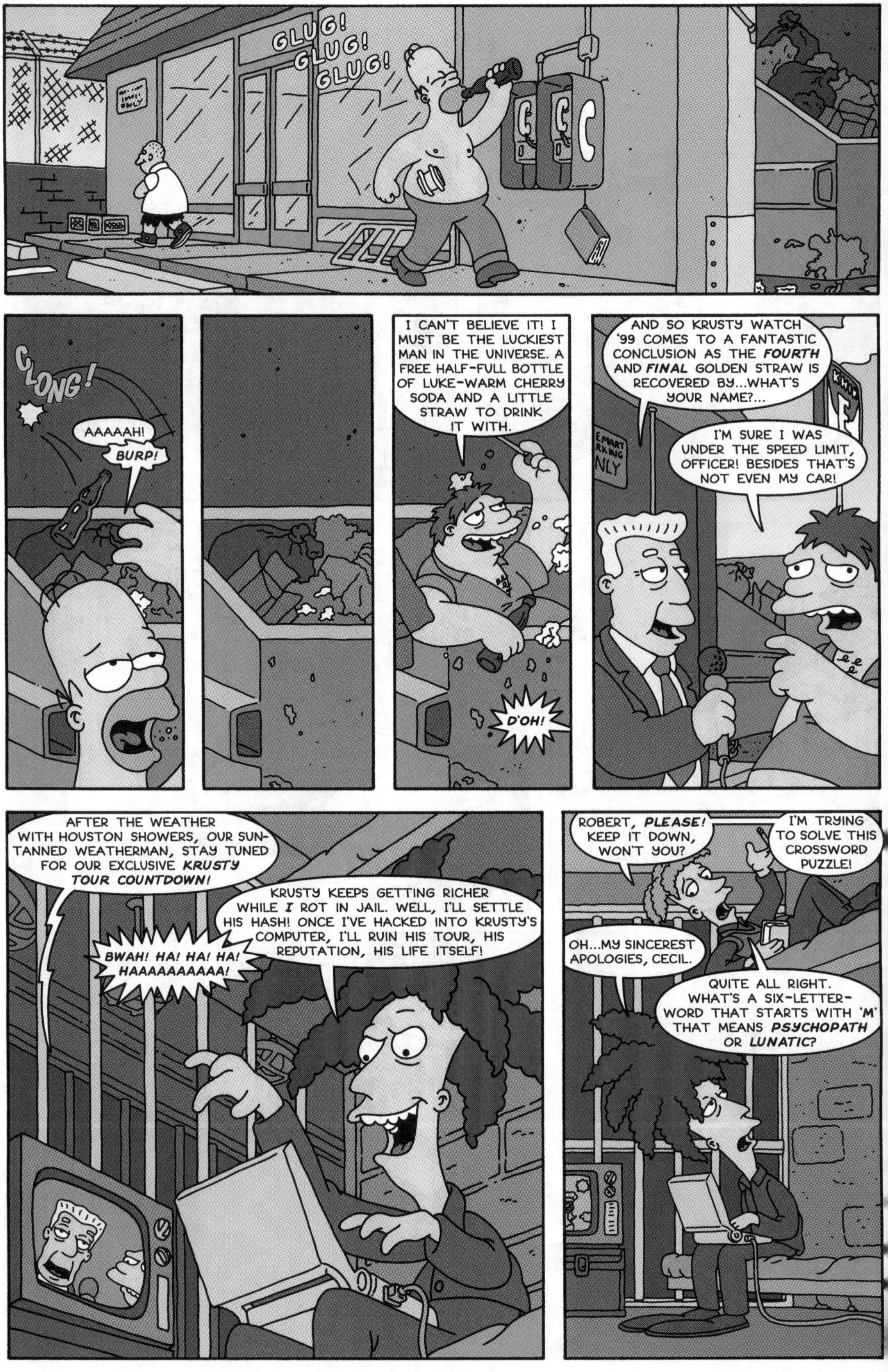

GLUG! GLUG! GLUG!
CLONG!
AAAAAH!
BURP!
I CAN'T BELIEVE IT! I MUST BE THE LUCKIEST MAN IN THE UNIVERSE. A FREE HALF-FULL BOTTLE OF LUKE-WARM CHERRY SODA AND A LITTLE STRAW TO DRINK IT WITH.
D'OH!
AND SO KRUSTY WATCH '99 COMES TO A FANTASTIC CONCLUSION AS THE FOURTH AND FINAL GOLDEN STRAW IS RECOVERED BY...WHAT'S YOUR NAME?...
I'M SURE I WAS UNDER THE SPEED LIMIT, OFFICER! BESIDES THAT'S NOT EVEN MY CAR!
AFTER THE WEATHER WITH HOUSTON SHOWERS, OUR SUN-TANNED WEATHERMAN, STAY TUNED FOR OUR EXCLUSIVE KRUSTY TOUR COUNTDOWN!
KRUSTY KEEPS GETTING RICHER WHILE I ROT IN JAIL. WELL, I'LL SETTLE HIS HASH! ONCE I'VE HACKED INTO KRUSTY'S COMPUTER, I'LL RUIN HIS TOUR, HIS REPUTATION, HIS LIFE ITSELF!
BWAH! HA! HA! HA! HAAAAAAAAAAA!
ROBERT, PLEASE! KEEP IT DOWN, WON'T YOU?
I'M TRYING TO SOLVE THIS CROSSWORD PUZZLE!
OH...MY SINCEREST APOLOGIES, CECIL.
QUITE ALL RIGHT. WHAT'S A SIX-LETTER-WORD THAT STARTS WITH 'M' THAT MEANS PSYCHOPATH OR LUNATIC?

PRISON
WELCOME TO THE KRUSTY BRAND FUN FACTORY PRE-TOUR EXTRAVAGANZA SHOW!
HI! I'M TROY MCCLURE. YOU MAY REMEMBER ME FROM OTHER PRE-TOUR EXTRAVAGANZAS LIKE "AN EVENING IN AL CAPONE'S VAULT" AND "SPELUNKING THROUGH HEF'S UNDERGROUND PLAYMATE GROTTO."
AND HERE ARE OUR FIRST LUCKY WINNERS, NELSON MUNTZ AND HIS PAROLE OFFICER, SNAKE.
COOL BADGE, MAN.
DUDE, YOU WOULD NOT BELIEVE WHAT I HAD TO GO THROUGH TO GET IT.
NEXT UP IS MR. BARNEY GUMBLE. SAY BARNEY, WHO'S THIS VISION OF LOVELINESS WITH YOU?
HELLO, I AM BARNEY'S MOTHER. YOU MAY CALL ME...BARNEY'S MOTHER.
I HAVEN'T BEEN THIS EXCITED SINCE BABY SHAMU WAS BORN. AND I'M NOT EVEN THE FA--
LOOK EVERYBODY, THE DOOR IS OPENING.

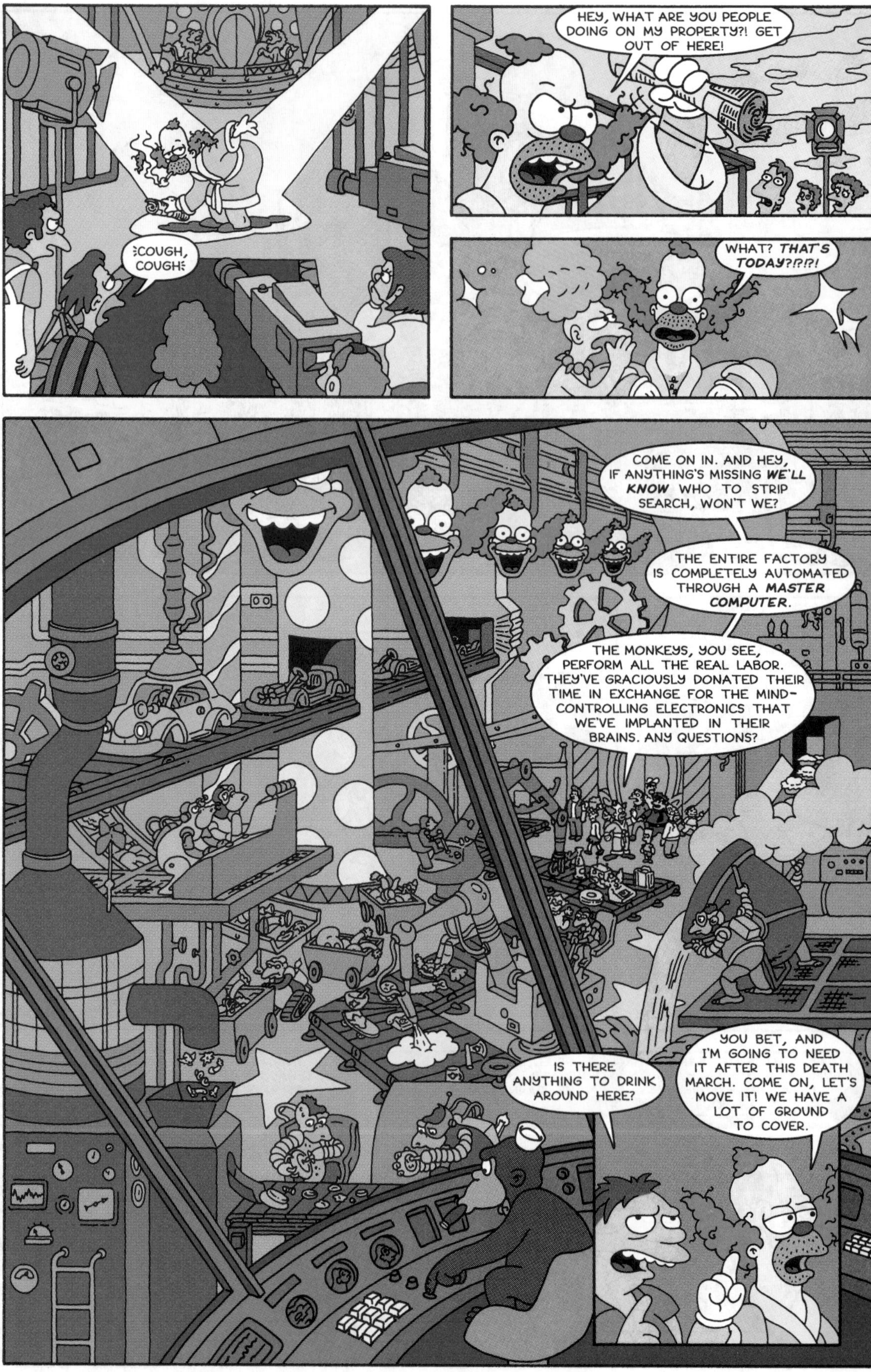

:COUGH, COUGH:
HEY, WHAT ARE YOU PEOPLE DOING ON MY PROPERTY?! GET OUT OF HERE!
WHAT? **THAT'S TODAY**?!?!?!
COME ON IN. AND HEY, IF ANYTHING'S MISSING **WE'LL KNOW** WHO TO STRIP SEARCH, WON'T WE?
THE ENTIRE FACTORY IS COMPLETELY AUTOMATED THROUGH A **MASTER COMPUTER**.
THE MONKEYS, YOU SEE, PERFORM ALL THE REAL LABOR. THEY'VE GRACIOUSLY DONATED THEIR TIME IN EXCHANGE FOR THE MIND-CONTROLLING ELECTRONICS THAT WE'VE IMPLANTED IN THEIR BRAINS. ANY QUESTIONS?
IS THERE ANYTHING TO DRINK AROUND HERE?
YOU BET, AND I'M GOING TO NEED IT AFTER THIS DEATH MARCH. COME ON, LET'S MOVE IT! WE HAVE A LOT OF GROUND TO COVER.

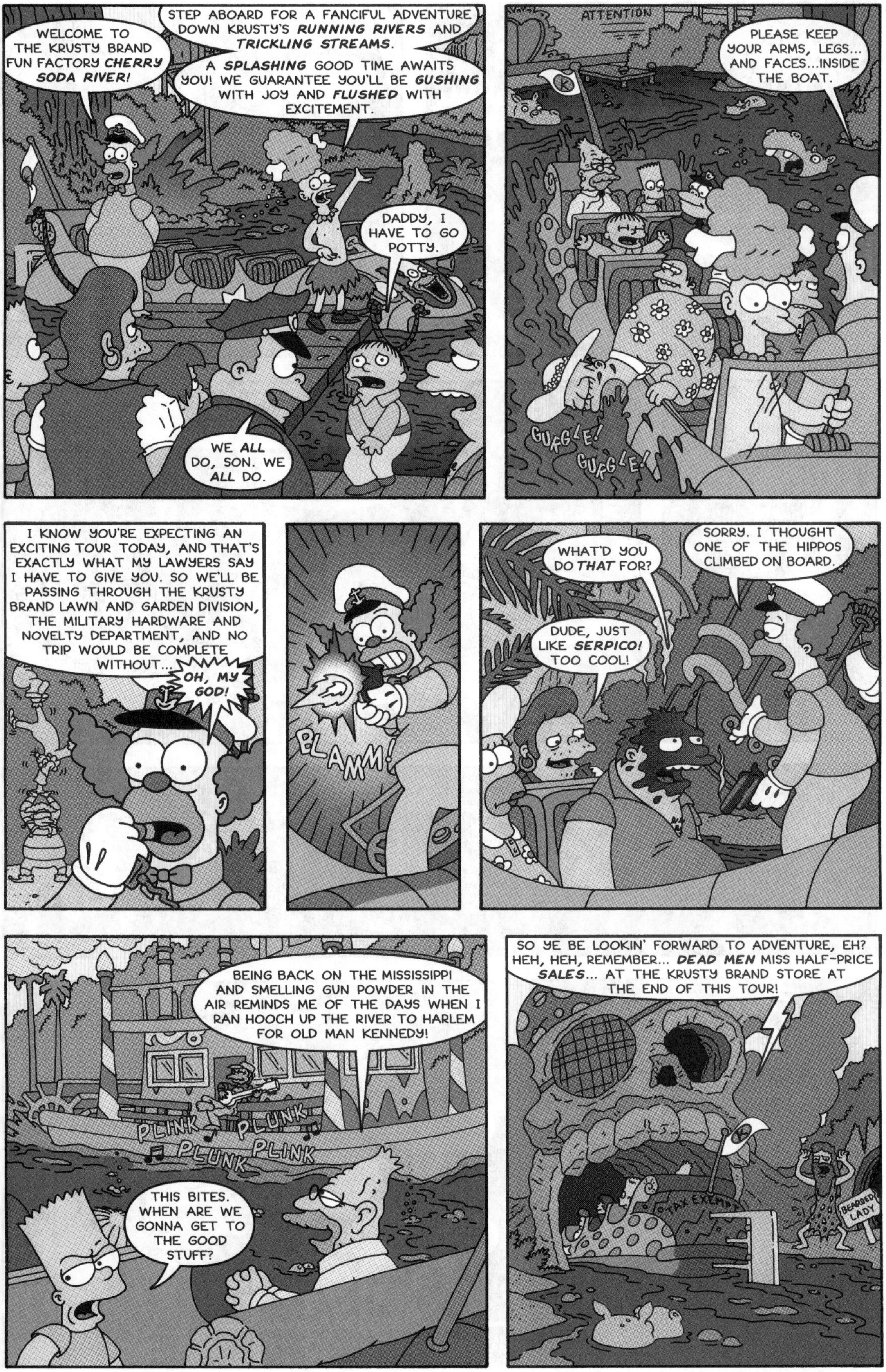
WELCOME TO THE KRUSTY BRAND FUN FACTORY CHERRY SODA RIVER!
STEP ABOARD FOR A FANCIFUL ADVENTURE DOWN KRUSTY'S RUNNING RIVERS AND TRICKLING STREAMS.
A SPLASHING GOOD TIME AWAITS YOU! WE GUARANTEE YOU'LL BE GUSHING WITH JOY AND FLUSHED WITH EXCITEMENT.
DADDY, I HAVE TO GO POTTY.
WE ALL DO, SON. WE ALL DO.
ATTENTION
PLEASE KEEP YOUR ARMS, LEGS... AND FACES...INSIDE THE BOAT.
GURGLE! GURGLE!
I KNOW YOU'RE EXPECTING AN EXCITING TOUR TODAY, AND THAT'S EXACTLY WHAT MY LAWYERS SAY I HAVE TO GIVE YOU. SO WE'LL BE PASSING THROUGH THE KRUSTY BRAND LAWN AND GARDEN DIVISION, THE MILITARY HARDWARE AND NOVELTY DEPARTMENT, AND NO TRIP WOULD BE COMPLETE WITHOUT...
OH, MY GOD!
BLAMM!
WHAT'D YOU DO THAT FOR?
SORRY. I THOUGHT ONE OF THE HIPPOS CLIMBED ON BOARD.
DUDE, JUST LIKE SERPICO! TOO COOL!
BEING BACK ON THE MISSISSIPPI AND SMELLING GUN POWDER IN THE AIR REMINDS ME OF THE DAYS WHEN I RAN HOOCH UP THE RIVER TO HARLEM FOR OLD MAN KENNEDY!
PLINK PLUNK PLUNK PLINK
THIS BITES. WHEN ARE WE GONNA GET TO THE GOOD STUFF?
SO YE BE LOOKIN' FORWARD TO ADVENTURE, EH? HEH, HEH, REMEMBER... DEAD MEN MISS HALF-PRICE SALES... AT THE KRUSTY BRAND STORE AT THE END OF THIS TOUR!
TAX EXEMPT
BEARDED LADY

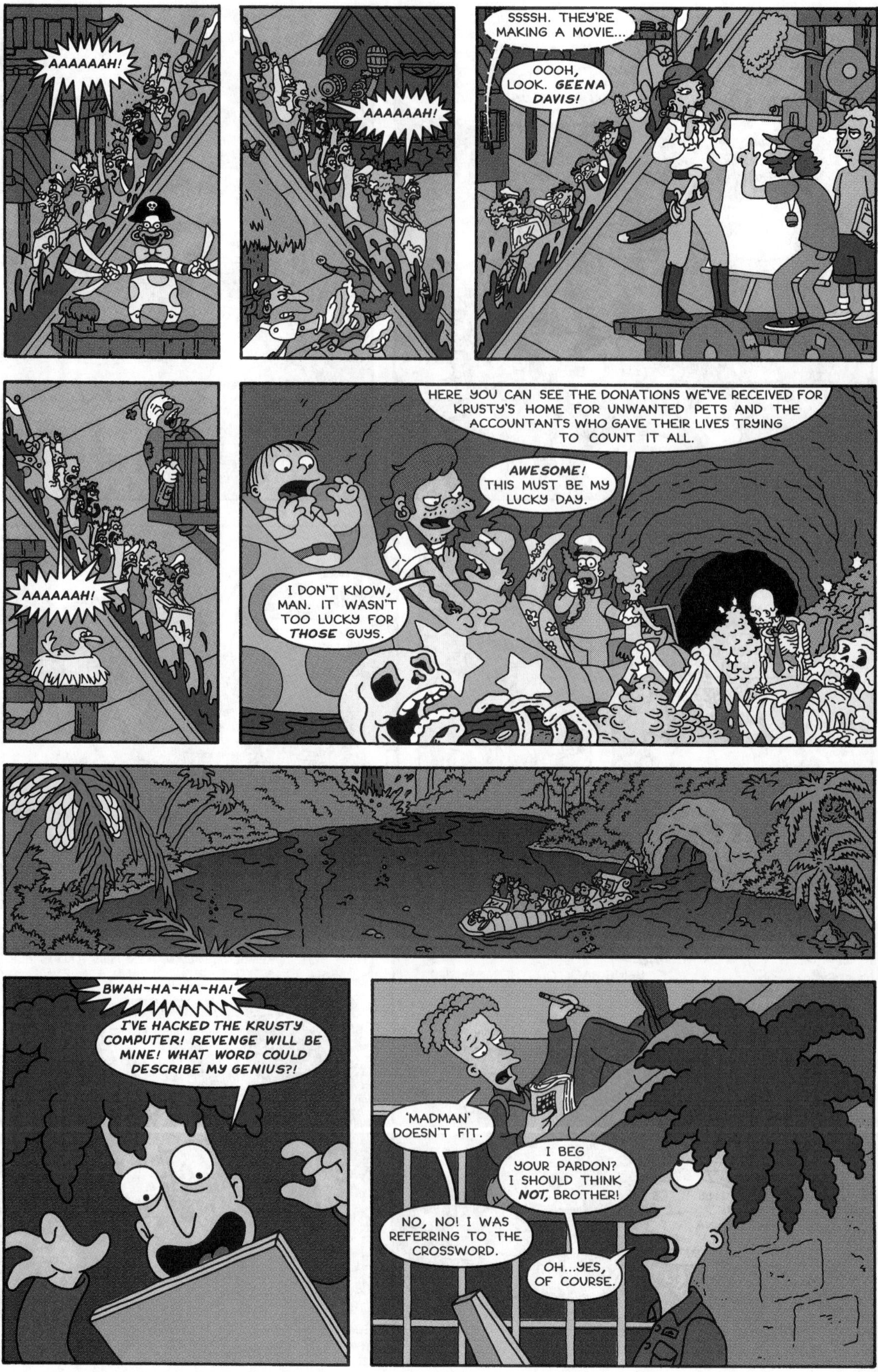
AAAAAAH!
AAAAAAH!
SSSSH. THEY'RE MAKING A MOVIE...
OOOH, LOOK. GEENA DAVIS!
AAAAAAH!
HERE YOU CAN SEE THE DONATIONS WE'VE RECEIVED FOR KRUSTY'S HOME FOR UNWANTED PETS AND THE ACCOUNTANTS WHO GAVE THEIR LIVES TRYING TO COUNT IT ALL.
AWESOME! THIS MUST BE MY LUCKY DAY.
I DON'T KNOW, MAN. IT WASN'T TOO LUCKY FOR THOSE GUYS.
BWAH-HA-HA-HA!
I'VE HACKED THE KRUSTY COMPUTER! REVENGE WILL BE MINE! WHAT WORD COULD DESCRIBE MY GENIUS?!
'MADMAN' DOESN'T FIT.
I BEG YOUR PARDON? I SHOULD THINK NOT, BROTHER!
NO, NO! I WAS REFERRING TO THE CROSSWORD.
OH...YES, OF COURSE.

CLICK!
OH, NO! SOMEONE'S RELEASED THE GIANT AFRICAN CHERRY THAT I USE TO FLAVOR MY CHERRY SODA.
MMMMM... GIANT AFRICAN CHERRY.
LOOKS LIKE WE'RE GOIN' DOWN, BOYS!
DUDE, THIS BLOWS!
DON'T WORRY! KRUSTY WILL SAVE US!
SORRY, FOLKS, THERE'S ONLY ROOM FOR ONE.
SCRUNCH!

I'M KING OF THE WORLD!
NO, WAIT... I'M GONNA DIE!
HEY, WHAT'S GOING ON?
IT'S THE NORTH POLE. WE'RE COMING SANTA! BREAK OUT THE EGG NOG!
SETTLE DOWN. SETTLE DOWN. I THINK THIS EXPLAINS EVERYTHING.
KRUSTY BRAND Frozen Food Division
OH, MAN. WHAT ROTTEN LUCK.
DUDE, WE'VE BEEN DITCHED BY THE CLOWN.
WE'RE LOST, AND IT'S COLD.
FROST
RIGHT, SO WHAT WE NEED TO DO IS GET OUR PRIORITIES STRAIGHT. I THINK WE NEED TO...EAT GRAMPA!
I CAN'T FEEL MY TOES.
EAT ME?!? WHY?!?!
FREON
SHEESH. LOOK AROUND DAD. WE'RE IN THE SNOW. WE'RE LOST. WE'VE GOT TO EAT SOMEBODY.
I KNOW THAT, YOU IDIOT. BUT WHY ON EARTH WOULD YOU WANT TO EAT A SCRAWNY OLD MAN?
LET'S EAT FAT BOY!
HEY!
TOO BAD WE DON'T HAVE ANY APPLESAUCE, DUDE.
HEH, HEH. NOW TAKE IT EASY. TAKE IT EASY.
I BET MY DADDY TASTES LIKE CHICKEN.

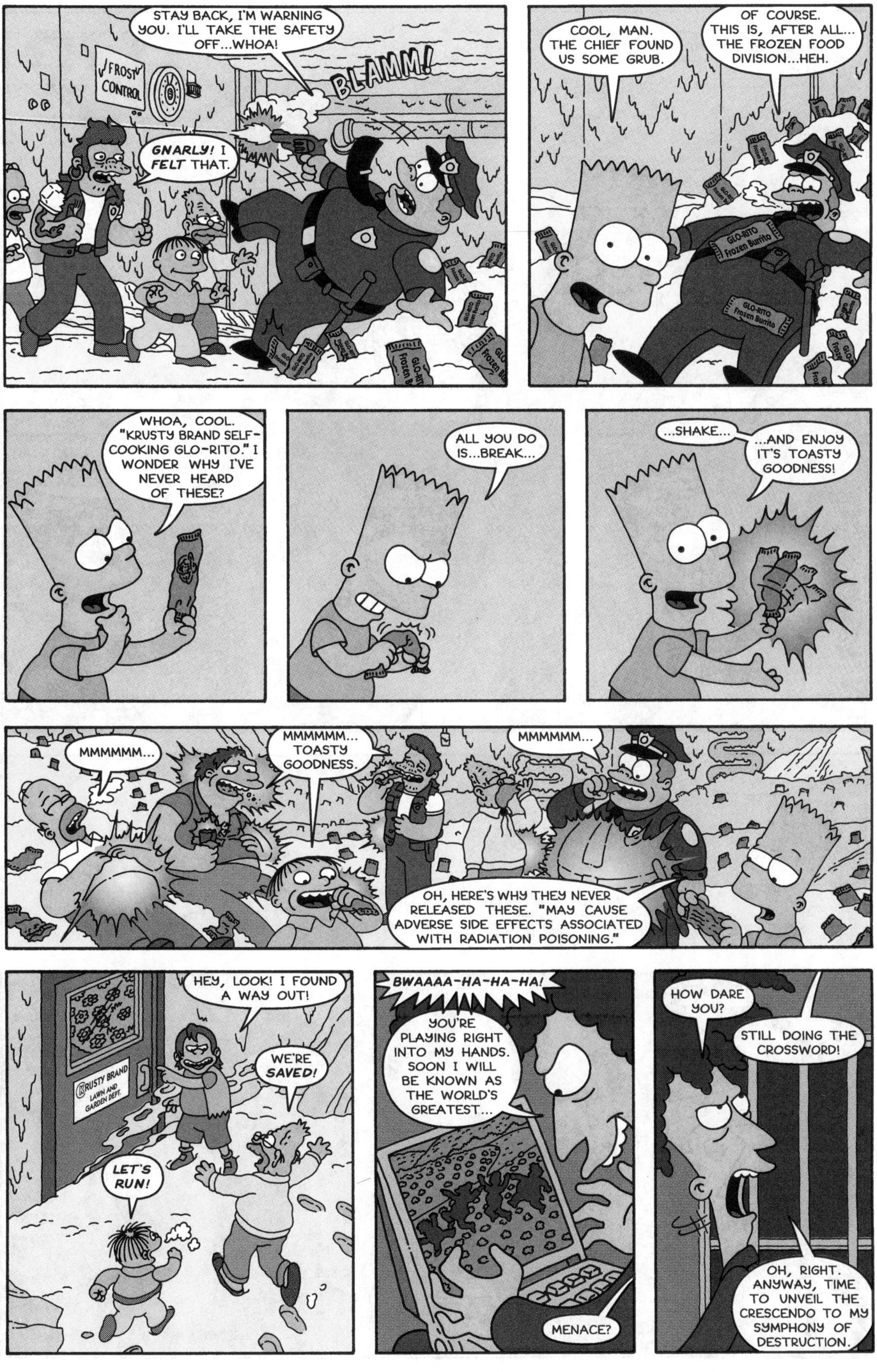
STAY BACK, I'M WARNING YOU. I'LL TAKE THE SAFETY OFF...WHOA!
BLAMM!
FROST CONTROL
GNARLY! I FELT THAT.
GLO-RITO Frozen Burrito
COOL, MAN. THE CHIEF FOUND US SOME GRUB.
OF COURSE. THIS IS, AFTER ALL... THE FROZEN FOOD DIVISION...HEH.
GLO-RITO Frozen Burrito
WHOA, COOL. "KRUSTY BRAND SELF-COOKING GLO-RITO." I WONDER WHY I'VE NEVER HEARD OF THESE?
ALL YOU DO IS...BREAK...
...SHAKE...
...AND ENJOY IT'S TOASTY GOODNESS!
MMMMMM...
MMMMMM... TOASTY GOODNESS.
MMMMMM...
OH, HERE'S WHY THEY NEVER RELEASED THESE. "MAY CAUSE ADVERSE SIDE EFFECTS ASSOCIATED WITH RADIATION POISONING."
HEY, LOOK! I FOUND A WAY OUT!
KRUSTY BRAND LAWN AND GARDEN DEPT.
WE'RE SAVED!
LET'S RUN!
BWAAAA-HA-HA-HA!
YOU'RE PLAYING RIGHT INTO MY HANDS. SOON I WILL BE KNOWN AS THE WORLD'S GREATEST...
MENACE?
HOW DARE YOU?
STILL DOING THE CROSSWORD!
OH, RIGHT. ANYWAY, TIME TO UNVEIL THE CRESCENDO TO MY SYMPHONY OF DESTRUCTION.

"...RELEASE THE MONKEYS!"
Lawn Spike Super Shooter
Weed Whacker
NOW, NOW, DON'T CRY, RALPHIE. HERE YOU CAN HOLD MY GUN. NO WAIT, THAT WOULD BE SILLY... I'LL GIVE YOU THE CUFFS.
WAAAAA!
I'VE GOT YOUR BACK, COPPER!
LET'S *DO* IT!
FREEZE, SCOFFLAWS!
BIF!
BAF!

WHACK!
HI-YA MONKEY DUDE!
PUNT!
PUNT!
PUNT!
OH, MY ACHING LUMBAGO.
WHAP!
HIGH-FIVE ME, COPPER!
THAT'S SOME NICE KICKIN' THERE, SNAKE.
ANYWAY...
HEH...
OOK! EEE! EEE!
YOU DON'T SCARE ME. I'VE SEEN "WHEN ANIMALS ATTACK" THIRTY-SEVEN TIMES.
BASH!
I'M GONNA GROW BIG AND STRONG.
FERTILIZER STRAIGHT FROM THE KING OF BS
IF CHUCK HESTON CAN WHIP YOUR BUTTS, SO CAN I!

I'M ALL OUT OF POTS. QUICK BOY, GIVE ME SOMETHING.
D'OH!
HA, HA!
YOU KNOW WHAT WOULD GO GOOD WITH THESE POPPIES? SOME NICE COLOMBIAN COFFEE.
TAKE *THAT,* YOU ROBO-BABOON!
BIF!
YOU DA MAN, HOMER.
HEH, HEH. I ALWAYS KNEW MY YEARS OF PRACTICE WOULD PAY OFF.
THANK YOU, SPRINGFIELD ZOO.

THERE'S TOO MANY OF THEM! THE TIME FOR BRUTE FORCE AND RAW COURAGE IS OVER. IT'S TIME FOR PLAN B!
WHAT'S PLAN B, HOMER?
RUN FOR IT!
D'OH! WHAT IDIOT PUT A CLIFF IN THE MIDDLE OF A POPPY FIELD?
PROBABLY THE SAME IDIOT THAT PUT A POPPY FIELD UNDERGROUND.
I HATE TO ASK THIS, DAD, BUT ARE WE GOING TO DIE?
WEED WHACKER
YOU LISTEN TO ME, BOY! I MAY NOT BE THE BEST DAD IN THE WORLD, I MAY NOT HAVE BEEN THERE EVERY TIME YOU NEEDED ME, BUT THERE'S NO WAY I'M GOING TO LET THESE MECHANICAL MONKEYS HURT YOU.
NOW, GET BEHIND ME, BOY!
WAAAH!
OOPS!

SHROOOOOM!
HEY, HEY!
COWABUNGA!
THANKS FOR NOT DYING, BOY. YOUR MOTHER WOULD HAVE BEEN PRETTY UPSET!
WHOOSH!
OOOK!
EEE!
OOOK!
EEE! EEE!
KRUSTY BRAND MILITARY HEADQUARTERS
WOO-HOO!
COOL JET, KRUSTY.
YEAH, BUT THE GOVERNMENT WON'T LET ME SELL 'EM. THEY LOOK TOO MUCH LIKE THE REAL THING ON THE STREET.
I CANCELED THE LINE WHEN THEY TOLD ME TO PUT SOME STUPID DAY-GLO CAPS ON THE NOSE.
EEP EEP! OOK OOK!
WHAT'S THAT BOY? TROUBLE AT THE OLD MILL?
SIDESHOW BOB? HACKED INTO MY COMPUTERS? TRIED TO RUIN THE WHOLE TOUR?
WHY CAN'T YOU SPEAK IN COMPLETE SENTENCES?

GEE, I'M SORRY, FOLKS. IT LOOKS LIKE SIDESHOW BOB RUINED THE DAY.
ARE YOU KIDDING, MAN? THIS WAS THE BEST TOUR EVER!
THAT WAS MORE FUN THAN THE TIME I WENT ON TOUR AT THE KRUSTY BRAND FUN FACTORY.
I ATE DIRT!
YEAH, BUT IT JUST TANS MY HIDE THAT SIDESHOW BOB GOT AWAY WITH IT.
I WISH THERE WAS SOME WAY I COULD GET BACK AT HIM.
THWAK!
UH-OH!
TAPPITY TAP-TAP!
CRASHH!
WHY, OH WHY CAN'T I LEAVE WELL ENOUGH ALONE? IT'S NOT MY FAULT I'M A...
MANIAC?
CECIL, REALLY!
NO, NO! IT'S THE CROSSWORD I WAS LOOKING FOR!
HEY, HEY! THAT'S ALL, FOLKS!
THAT'S SOME NICE PAYBACK THERE, MR. K.
THE END

The Day the NAGGING Stopped

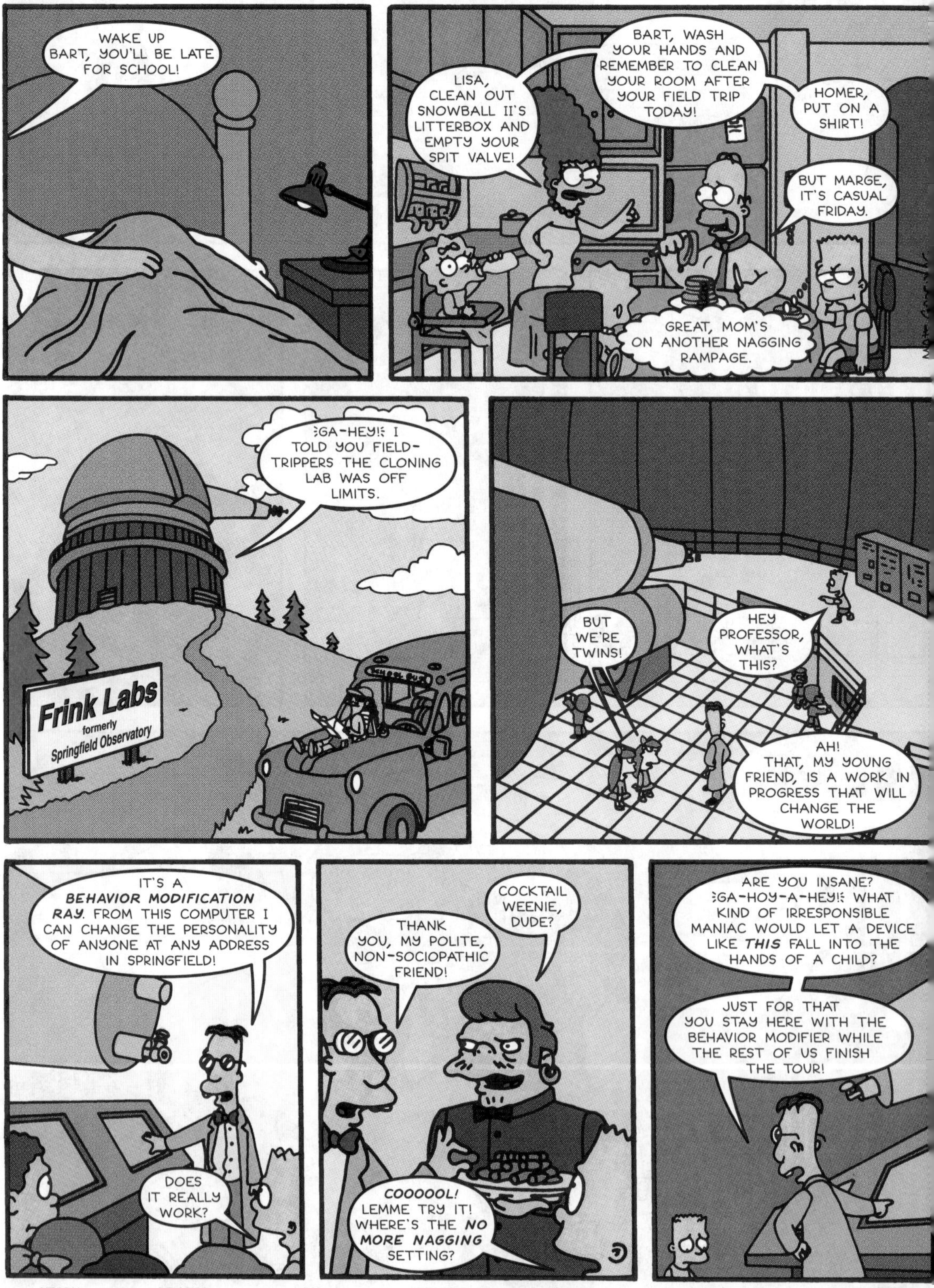

STORY	PENCILS	INKS	LETTERS	COLORS	EDITOR	NITPICKER
IAN BOOTHBY	JULIUS PREITE	TIM HARKINS	KAREN BATES	CHRIS UNGAR	BILL MORRISON	MATT GROENING

SOON...
HERE GOES!
742 EVERGREEN TERRACE
NAGGING
PRESS HERE
BEHAVIOR RAYS FOR DUMMIES
VREEEP!
LATER...
UH...MOM? I'M HOME! IS THERE ANYTHING YOU'D LIKE ME TO DO?
YES, GO OUT AND PLAY! HERE'S MONEY FOR ICE CREAM.
THANKS!
IT WORKED! NO MORE CHORES EVER! THANK YOU ETHICALLY QUESTIONABLE SCIENCE!
HEY BART, Y'KNOW WHAT THEY SAY, WHEN MORE THAN A FOOT OF GRASS IS SHOWIN' THAT'S THE TIME YOU SHOULD BE MOWIN'!
NOTE TO SELF: USE RAY ON FLANDERS.
UH...THANKS.
HEY GUYS! ICE CREAM IS ON ME!
I DON'T KNOW, BART. DO YOU REALLY THINK YOU DESERVE ICE CREAM WITH YOUR ROOM SO MESSY?
BNL

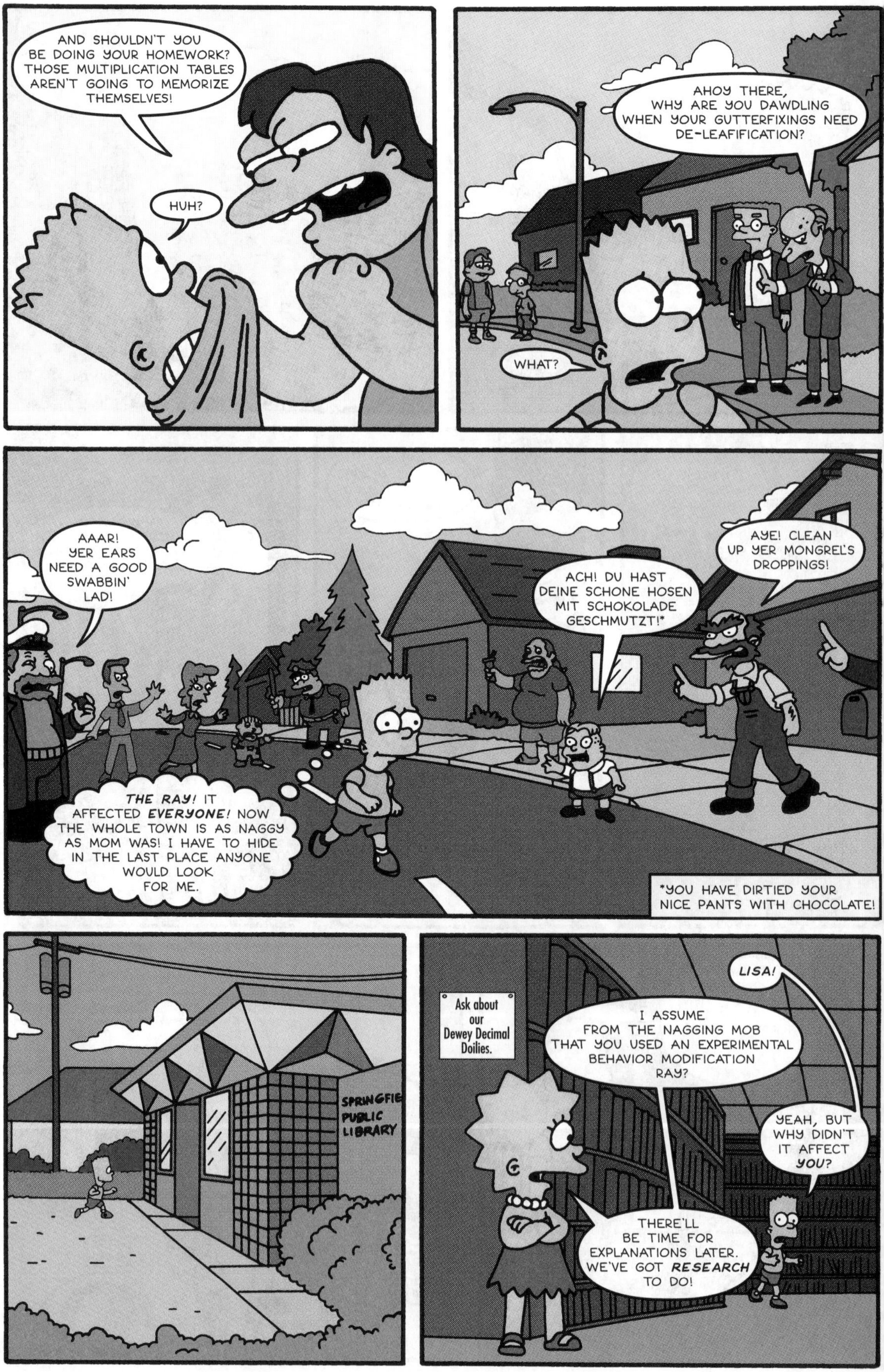

AND SHOULDN'T YOU BE DOING YOUR HOMEWORK? THOSE MULTIPLICATION TABLES AREN'T GOING TO MEMORIZE THEMSELVES!
HUH?
AHOY THERE, WHY ARE YOU DAWDLING WHEN YOUR GUTTERFIXINGS NEED DE-LEAFIFICATION?
WHAT?
AAAR! YER EARS NEED A GOOD SWABBIN' LAD!
ACH! DU HAST DEINE SCHONE HOSEN MIT SCHOKOLADE GESCHMUTZT!*
AYE! CLEAN UP YER MONGREL'S DROPPINGS!
THE RAY! IT AFFECTED EVERYONE! NOW THE WHOLE TOWN IS AS NAGGY AS MOM WAS! I HAVE TO HIDE IN THE LAST PLACE ANYONE WOULD LOOK FOR ME.
*YOU HAVE DIRTIED YOUR NICE PANTS WITH CHOCOLATE!
SPRINGFIE PUBLIC LIBRARY
Ask about our Dewey Decimal Doilies.
LISA!
I ASSUME FROM THE NAGGING MOB THAT YOU USED AN EXPERIMENTAL BEHAVIOR MODIFICATION RAY?
YEAH, BUT WHY DIDN'T IT AFFECT YOU?
THERE'LL BE TIME FOR EXPLANATIONS LATER. WE'VE GOT RESEARCH TO DO!

WHAT CAN I DO TO STOP THEM?
THE ONLY WAY TO BREAK THE NAGGING CYCLE IS TO DO ALL YOUR CHORES AND MAKE SURE YOU'RE CLEAN AND PRESENTABLE.
THERE'S GOT TO BE SOME OTHER...
KRASH!
UNPOPULAR SCIENCE MAGAZINE
ALPHABETIZE YOUR COMIC COLLECTION!
CRASH!
CLEAN UP THIS GLASS WE JUST BROKE!
RUN HOME BART! CLEAN, TIDY, AND SANITIZE FOR YOUR OWN PROTECTION!
HOURS LATER...
IT'S DONE! ALL ***DONE!*** ALL ***CLEAN!*** THIS IS HORRIBLE, LIKE SOME KIND OF ***NIGHTMARE***...
WAX
"A NIGHTMARE..."
"NIGHTMARE..."
WAKE UP, YOU'LL BE LATE FOR SCHOOL.
DARN IT MOTHER! I WAS HAVING THE MOST WONDERFUL DREAM!
AW, QUIT YOUR BELLYACHING, CLEAN YOUR ROOM AND GET TO SCHOOL.
YES, MOTHER!
THE END

BONGO COMICS GROUP
SIMPSONS™
COMICS
#42
US $2.50
CAN $3.50
APPROVED BY THE COMICS CODE AUTHORITY
Duff
LIVE
CORE MELTDOWN IN PROGRESS
TOWN!!
the HOMER show
GROENING
©1999 BONGO ENTERTAINMENT, INC. THE SIMPSONS ©&TM TWENTIETH CENTURY FOX FILM CORPORATION. ALL RIGHTS RESERVED.

THE HOMER SHOW

SCRIPT CHUCK DIXON · *PENCILS* PHIL ORTIZ · *INKS* TIM BAVINGTON · *LETTERS* JEANNINE BLACK · *COLORS* NATHAN KANE · *MR. TELEVISION* MATT GROENING

WE GOT A TAPE OF THIS GUY ON *FIRE* LAST WEEK.
WASN'T HE THE ONE WHO GOT HIS HAND CAUGHT IN THE TELLER MACHINE ON "WORLD'S FUNNIEST SURVEILLANCE VIDEOS?"
I THINK WE HAVE A *LOT* OF THIS GUY ON TAPE.
HERE'S ONE. "GUY CRASHES LAWNMOWER INTO BEEHIVE."
HERE'S ANOTHER ONE. "GUY WITH LIPS CAUGHT IN FAN."
AND "GUY WITH MONKEY IN PANTS."
FUNNY
SUCKS
WE GET TAPES OF THIS CLOWN EVERY WEEK.
SO WHAT DOES THIS MEAN?
THAT THIS GUY IS THE *DUMBEST* MOPE EVER CAUGHT ON VIDEO.
THAT HE'S CAPABLE OF FEATS OF *STUPIDITY* UNSEEN BEFORE IN CIVILIZATION.
THAT HE'S THE *HOLY GRAIL* OF ASININE BEHAVIOR.
THAT A *STAR* IS BORN!

DUMBUBBY H'EP NEE!
H'EP NEEEEEEE!
GENIUS. PURE GENIUS!
I THINK BUILDING A NEW SHOW AROUND THIS GOOF IS A FABULOUS IDEA!
WE ALREADY HAVE ENOUGH FOOTAGE OF THIS HOMER SIMPSON TO FILL TEN PROGRAMMING HOURS.
BUT I FEEL WE'LL NEED MORE. LOTS MORE.
WE CAN'T RELY ON OUR VIEWERS SENDING IN RANDOM TAPES OF THIS MEGA-TALENT.
BUT THAT'S HOW WE DO ALL OUR SHOWS--FROM "WHEN PETS GO POSTAL" TO "WORLD'S ZANIEST POLICE CHASES."
TRY TO THINK OUTSIDE THE BOX, JEFF.
IF THIS HOMER SIMPSON GENERATES THIS MUCH TAPE ON AN IRREGULAR BASIS, IMAGINE WHAT THE CAMERA DOESN'T CATCH.
I PROPOSE WE FOLLOW THIS MAN TWENTY FOUR-HOURS A DAY.
I HAVE SO MUCH FAITH IN HOMER SIMPSON'S TOTAL LACK OF SENSE AND COORDINATION, THAT I'M WILLING TO BUILD THE NEW FALL SEASON AROUND HIM.
THE HOMER SHOW
Only on FOX!

I'M SOLD ON THIS. IT'S GOING TO BE BIG. URKEL BIG.
I'M OPEN TO SUGGESTIONS FOR WHERE TO PLACE "THE HOMER SHOW" ON THE SCHEDULE.
WE COULD ALWAYS PUT IT IN MILLENNIUM'S SLOT.
HUH?
UNNH!
THWAK!
OKAY. LET'S SCRAMBLE PEOPLE. WE HAVE A MID-SIZED CITY TO WIRE BY MONDAY!

ER, AH, YOU HOLLYWOOD SHARPIES HAVE TAKEN ADVANTAGE OF US BEFORE.
I SAY WE ARE NOT RUBES HERE IN SPRINGFIELD.
MAYOR QUIMBY
SPRINGFIELD
SOFT MONEY
THE CREW FROM "RADIOACTIVE MAN: THE MOVIE" GOT OUT OF TOWN WITHOUT PAYING THE CROISSANT TAX.
THOSE WERE *MOVIE* PEOPLE, MAYOR QUIMBY.
A BUNCH OF IMMORAL PREDATORS.
WE'RE IN *TELEVISION*, YOUR HONOR.
ER, A LITTLE TO THE LEFT, INGA.
ER, AH, WHAT'S THE DIFFERENCE?
WE'RE AMORAL PREDATORS, MR. MAYOR.
NO...
MOTHER OF GOD, IT *CAN'T* BE!

SAY IT AIN'T SO, MOE...
SAY IT AIN'T *SO*!
MOE'S
CLOSED
~~DEATH IN FAMILY~~
~~ILLNESS~~
~~HEALTH DEPARTMENT~~
~~GENERAL ENNUI~~
JUST GO HOME!
WELL, IF THAT'S THE KIND OF ESTABLISHMENT YOU'RE RUNNING, SZYSLAK, I'LL JUST TAKE MY BUSINESS TO--
2714
BLOATERS AT THE SQUIDPORT
D'OH!
CLOSED
BLOATERS AT THE SQUIDPOR
WELL, I KNOW ONE PLACE I CAN ALWAYS COUNT ON TO BE--
-E-MART
WE NEVER CLOSE
EXCEPT FOR TONIGHT
HOW MUCH CAN ONE MAN TAKE?
HAS THE WORLD GONE *MAD?*

WELL, THAT LEAVES ONLY ONE PLACE FOR A WORKING MAN TO GO.
HOME.
8-TRAC
HEY, WHERE ARE YOU GUYS GOING?
WE'RE GOIN' TO THE BIG TOWN MEETIN', HOMER.
DUMMY! HE'S NOT SUPPOSED TO KNOW.
WHAT TOWN MEETING?
UH, I DIDN'T MEAN TO SAY THAT. IT'S MY CONDITION.
YEAH, HE'S GOT AN UNCONTROLLABLE IMPULSE TO TALK ABOUT NON-EXISTENT TOWN MEETINGS.
THEY DID A TV MOVIE ABOUT IT LAST MONTH.
I THINK MARGE SAW THAT ONE.
BIG TOWN MEETING TO-NITE!
NO PARKING
El Barto
SEE YA AT THE PLANT, HOMER.
SURE.
SEE YA.

WE'RE SORRY TO HAVE CALLED THE ENTIRE POPULATION OF SPRINGFIELD TO THIS MEETING TONIGHT.
MAN, WHAT A TURNOUT. ARE THESE MEETINGS *USUALLY* THIS WELL ATTENDED?
WE'RE HERE 'CAUSE WE HEARD YOU GOT A BUTTLOAD OF *CASH* TO THROW AROUND.
OH.
WELL, THEN LET'S GET RIGHT TO THE POINT.
TWO HOURS LATER...
...AND SO WE'LL BE WIRING THE ENTIRE TOWN FOR VIDEO.
BUT SECRECY IS OF THE *UTMOST* IMPORTANCE. *NONE* OF THE SIMPSON FAMILY MUST KNOW THAT HOMER SIMPSON IS BEING TAPED.
AND EXACTLY *HOW* DO *WE* BENEFIT FROM THIS?
THE FOX TELEVISION NETWORK WILL PAY FOR THE CONSTRUCTION OF A COMMUNITY ARTS CENTER.
OR WE COULD JUST THROW A BUTTLOAD OF *CASH* AROUND.

LIBERTY AND JUSTICE FOR ALL
SPRINGFIELD COUNTY COURT HOUSE
YAAAAAAAAAAAY!
DID YOU HEAR THAT?
HUH?
IT SOUNDED LIKE CHEERING.
PROBABLY THE FLANDERSES, MARGE. THEY'RE ALWAYS CHEERING ABOUT GOD OR SIN OR SOMETHING.
HMMMM...
HOW WAS YOUR DAY, HOMEY?
OKAY, I GUESS. EXCEPT FOR EVERY STORE DOWNTOWN BEING CLOSED FOR NO GOOD REASON.
THE SMOKE DETECTOR INSPECTORS WERE HERE.
YEAH?
THEY MADE THE KIDS AND ME LEAVE THE HOUSE FOR HOURS WHILE THEY CHECKED OUR BATTERIES.
THEY WERE VERY NICE ABOUT IT, BUT I HAVE A FUNNY FEELING...
ZZZZZZZZZ...
GOOD NIGHT, HOMER.
YEAH. GOODNIGHT, HOMER.

HOW'S OUR LATEST HIT, GENTLEMEN?
BEAUTIFUL, CHIEF.
THIS GUY'S AN ARTIST.
LET'S SEE WHAT YOU'VE GOT, BOYS.
HE CUT HIMSELF SHAVING.
D'OH!
THEN HE DID THIS TO STOP THE BLEEDING.
THIS'LL STOP IT...
THEN HE FELL DOWN THE STAIRS.
WHOAP!
AND IT'S NOT EVEN NINE IN THE MORNING?
HA HA HA!
HA
LOOK! HE JUST STABBED HIMSELF WITH A BUTTER KNIFE!
HA!
HA HA HA!
WAY TO BE, HOMER.
MAYBE HE SHOULD HAVE HIS OWN CHANNEL!

GOOD MORNING TO YOU, MY VERY SPECIAL FRIEND!
HOW MAY I BE OF SERVICE TO YOU, VALUED CUSTOMER?
I DON'T KNOW WHAT I'M IN THE MOOD FOR.
WHATEVER THAT IS, MR. HOMER, YOUR EVERY OPTION IS A GOOD ONE.
EACH NUTRITIOUS SNACK AT THE KWIK-E-MART, ON SPRINGFIELD'S FAMOUS GOLDEN MILE, IS PACKED WITH TASTINESS AND A SHELF-LIFE WHICH IS EXTRA-LONG.
KRISPIE K
I'LL TAKE THE MONOSODIUM GLUTIMUNCHIES.
I HAVE ALSO PORKERJACKS AND TWELVE FLAVORS OF SQUISHEE INCLUDING JALAPEÑO MOCHA.
MMMMM... PORKERJACKS.
TANDOORI BURRITOS 2 FOR $1
PLEASE COME AGAIN TO THE KWIK-E-MART, WHERE VALUE MEANS ONLY PAYING TWICE AS MUCH!
THIS GUY'S DOIN' A COMMERCIAL.
FOR ALL THE GOOD IT'LL DO HIM. THE SHOW'S GONNA BE BLACKED OUT IN SPRINGFIELD.
WHAT'RE THEY SHOWING IN ITS PLACE?
STAY TUNED FOR AN ENCORE PRESENTATION OF MILLENNIUM.
AW, MAN...
SEE WHAT ELSE IS ON, BART.

AH, THE CLASSICS.
♫ THE ITCHY ♪ AND SCRATCHY SHOOOOOW... ♫
ITCHY & SCRATCHY
ITCHY & SCRATCHY in
SHAVING PRIVATE SCRATCHY
YANK!
KA-BOOM!
HA! HA HA HA! HA HA
HA
MINE FIELD
HA HA HA!

THE OVERNIGHTS ARE IN, PEOPLE.
THE HOMER SHOW IS A SMASH!
RATINGS
WHUMP!
WE'RE NUMBER ONE WITH MALES EIGHTEEN TO THIRTY-FOUR!
WE'RE NUMBER ONE WITH CONVICTED WHITEWATER CONSPIRATORS!
WE'RE NUMBER ONE WITH RECENT STATE LOTTERY WINNERS!
WE'RE NUMBER ONE WITH LARRY KING'S EX-WIVES!
THE ONLY DOWNSIDE IS IN OUR OPERATING BUDGET.
WE INSTALLED A THOUSAND CAMERAS IN SPRINGFIELD WHEN WE COULD HAVE COVERED HOMER SIMPSON'S WHOLE LIFE WITH JUST SIX.
FICTIO
BOOK CHECK-OUT DESK
Days without activity: 123.
SPRINGFIELD PUBLIC LIBRARY
HERE'S TO HOMER SIMPSON!
LONG MAY HE SCREW UP!
...AND THEN I SAID TO THAT GUY, "OH YEAH? SAYS YOU!!"
Duff BEER

THAT'S TELLIN' 'EM, HOMER!
WAY T'GO, SIMPSON.
DON RICKLES COULD NOT HAFF TOLD HIM OFF ANY BETTAH.
CAN I SAY "HI" TO MY MOM?
SLAP!
AND NOTHIN' GOES WITH A FINE ANECDOTE--
--LIKE DUFF BEER AND MOE'S TAVERN!
IT WAS GREAT, MARGE. EVERYONE AT MOE'S WAS HANGING ON MY EVERY WORD. I FELT LIKE... A PRIMA BALLERINA!
PRAISE FROM A BUNCH OF BARFLIES IS HARDLY ANYTHING TO BE PROUD OF.
SO WHAT MADE YOU THE LIFE OF THE PARTY ALL OF A SUDDEN?
I THINK EVERYONE HAS FINALLY GROWN TO APPRECIATE MY SOPHISTICATION AND URBANE WIT.
SNORT!
HEY...
HEE HEE
HA!
HA!
HA!
HEE HEE HEE!
HA!

AS WEEKS GO BY, HOMER SIMPSON BECOMES A NATIONAL OBSESSION.
TV
Fox's (not so) brightest star
GOD
NEWSWEEKLY MONTHLY
IT'S HIP TO BE A "D'OHP"!
THE NATIONAL CONSPIRER
Aliens Stole Homer's Brain-- and brought it BACK!
HOLLYWOOD INSIDER
DOOFUS IS BOFFO IN SYNDIE-INDIE DEAL.
HE SHOULD BE LEAVING THE HOUSE ANY MINUTE.
HOW MANY TIMES HAS HE RUN OVER THE MAILBOX?
THE VERMINATORS PEST CONTROL
THE SIMPSONS
THIS WEEK? FOUR.
BAM!
THAT'S FRANKIE BACK WITH THE DONUTS.
YOU'RE NOT FRANKIE.
IT WASN'T ME! THIS ISN'T EVEN MY BALL!
WHOA-HO-HE!
YOU'RE WATCHING OUR HOUSE!
$#@&!

SO, WHAT IS IT YOU WANT, KID? A NEW BIKE?
HA! DON'T MAKE ME LAUGH.
REMEMBER I COULD BLOW THIS WHOLE THING WITH ONE WORD TO MY DAD.
SO WHAT DO YOU WANT, BART?
I WANT ONE OF THOSE PHONY BALONEY HOLLYWOOD JOBS WITH NO WORK AND A FAT PAYCHECK.
WHAT'S THIS ABOUT?
BARTHOLOMEW J. SIMPSON EXECUTIVE PRODUCER
THAT'S ON A NEED-TO-KNOW BASIS, LIS'.
LIFE JUST ISN'T THE SAME, BARN. EVERYTHING'S CHANGED.
I HADN'T NOTICED, HOMER.
NOT FOR YOU. JUST FOR ME. THE WORLD IS A STRANGE PLACE.
WHATTA YA TALKIN' ABOUT, HOMER?
NOTHIN'S CHANGED HERE AT MOE'S.
I FEEL LIKE I'M BEING WATCHED.
DRINK Duff
IT'S ALL IN YOUR HEAD. LOOK AROUND YOU.
EEEEEEEEEK!

GOTTA GO HOME.
EVERYTHING'S NORMAL THERE.
MOE'S
HOMER!
HEY HOMER!
STAY AWAY!
IT'S HOMER!
YO HOMER!
WAIT HOMER!
HOMER BAY-BEE!
YAAAAAAAAH!
GOTTA GET HOME TO MARGE!
MARGE WILL KNOW WHAT TO DO.
JUST HAVE TO GET TO MY CAR.
GOOD ONE.
THE VERMINATORS PEST CONTROL
I DUNNO...
BASH!
...SOMETHING'S NOT RIGHT HERE.
MARGE!

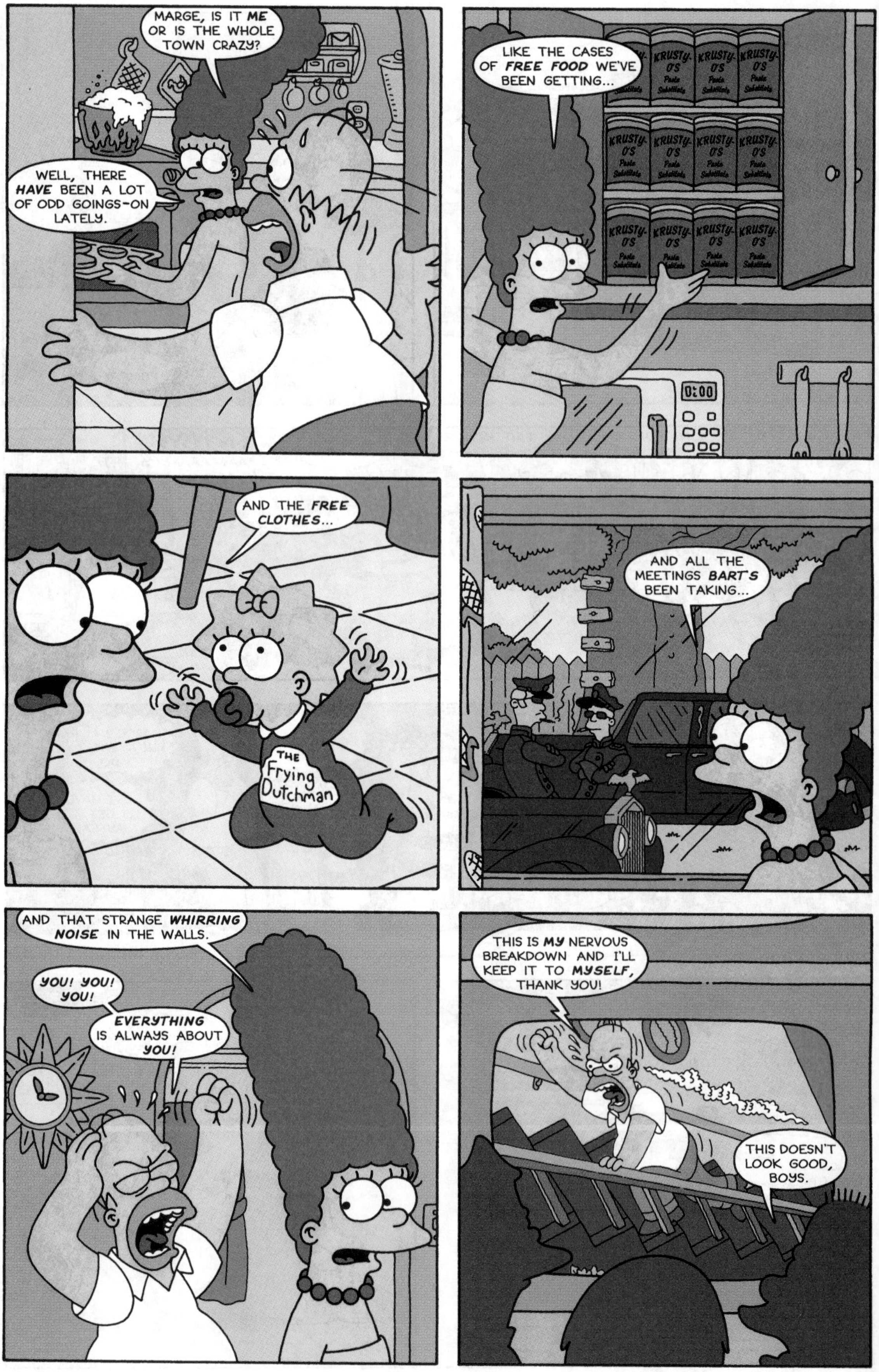
MARGE, IS IT ME OR IS THE WHOLE TOWN CRAZY?
WELL, THERE HAVE BEEN A LOT OF ODD GOINGS-ON LATELY.
LIKE THE CASES OF FREE FOOD WE'VE BEEN GETTING...
KRUSTY-O'S Pasta Substitute
AND THE FREE CLOTHES...
THE Frying Dutchman
AND ALL THE MEETINGS BART'S BEEN TAKING...
AND THAT STRANGE WHIRRING NOISE IN THE WALLS.
YOU! YOU! YOU!
EVERYTHING IS ALWAYS ABOUT YOU!
THIS IS MY NERVOUS BREAKDOWN AND I'LL KEEP IT TO MYSELF, THANK YOU!
THIS DOESN'T LOOK GOOD, BOYS.

HOMER'S BEEN IN BED FIVE DAYS IN A ROW, SIR.
HE HASN'T BUDGED.
HUNDREDS OF HOURS OF TAPE ALL LIKE THIS.
OUR ENTIRE SCHEDULE RESTS ON THIS SHOW.
I HAD HOPED IT WOULDN'T COME TO THIS, BUT SOMETHING'S GOT TO BE DONE!
SOON...
AND SO I'VE COME TO APPEAL DIRECTLY TO YOU, MR. SIMPSON.
FOX
WITHOUT YOUR KNOWING IT, AMERICA HAS COME TO LOVE YOU.
NOT IN SPITE OF YOUR FAULTS BUT BECAUSE OF THEM. AMERICA'S NOT LAUGHING AT YOU, HOMER. IT'S LAUGHING ABOUT YOU.
THIS COUNTRY, AND THIS NETWORK, NEED YOU TO CONTINUE YOUR SENSELESS BEHAVIOR AND RECKLESS DISREGARD FOR YOUR OWN DIGNITY.
CAN YOU DO IT, HOMER? FOR YOUR MILLIONS OF FANS?
YOU CAN COUNT ON ME!

AND SO IN THE ENSUING DAYS...
OH NO! I'M WEARING A LADIES' HAT!
HARDWARE
SECTOR 7G
OH! OH! I'VE FALLEN AND I CAN'T GET UP!
THEN THE POLAR BEAR SAYS TO THE RABBI...
ONE MORE JOKE AND I MUST KILL YOU, MR. HOMER.
Duff BEER SALE!
OOPS!
LOOKS LIKE I FORGOT MY PANTS AGAIN!
WHAT'S HE DOING?
GOOD LORD, HE'S--
--TRYING TO BE FUNNY.
WHY DID WE EVER LIKE THIS SHOW?
PUT ON THE WEATHER CHANNEL!
THE NASHVILLE NETWORK!
TURN IT OFF, EVEN!
THE BOTTOM FIVE SHOWS
151 FLY FISHING WITH HAL
152 MONKEYS BOWLING
153 LET ME TELL YOU ABOUT MY SURGERY
154 MILLENNIUM
155 THE HOMER SHOW

NOT MY BIGSCREEN!
NOT MY SECRETARY!
NOT MY LATTE MACHINE!
CAN'T WE NEGOTIATE?
THANKS A LOT, HOMER.
YOU EVEN BUNGLED BEING A BUNGLER.
FAME ISN'T EVERYTHING, BOY.
AS THE GREAT WORDSMITH, PAT SAJAK, ONCE SAID...
"ALL GLORY IS FLEETING." NOW, INSTEAD OF SHARING MY ZANY ANTICS WITH THE WORLD, I'LL JUST SHARE THEM WITH MY FAM--
Duff BEER
D'OH!
MMPH!
MMPH!
THE VERMINATORS PEST CONTROL
OCH!
ABC WILL PAY A FORTUNE FOR THIS!
THE END

CLASSICS
Illustrative
No. 49
SLOBBERWACKY
DUFF
SURLY

SLOBBERWACKY
'Twas Wiggum, and his slimy rogues,
SPRINGFIELD ANNUAL PICNIC
Springfield Shopper
STOLEN DUFF TRUCK STILL MISSING
Did cheat to win the three-leg'd race:
BLAM!
BLAM!
THAT'S SOME GOOD DIVERTIN' THERE LOU!
THANKS, CHIEF!
BLAM!
All tipsy were the friends of Moe,
I WONDER WHERE BARNEY IS? IT'S NOT LIKE HIM TO MISS ALL THE EXCITEMENT.
And Nelson stole third base.
H-HEY! BRING THAT BACK! WE NEED IT!
HA, HA!
"Beware the Slobberwack, my son! The jaws that drool, the paunch that sags!
OH, MAN! THE ONLY THING TO FEAR AROUND HERE IS YOUR BREATH, HOME-BOY!

Beware the Jub-Jub beast, and shun...
CONSARN IT! I NEED THOSE FOR MY COB CORN!
...Jub-Jub's owners, the sister-hags!"
HMMPH!
AND YOU WONDER WHERE HOMER GETS IT FROM!
HELP! HELLLP!
Bart took his trusty sling in hand:
THAT'S IT! I'M OUTTA HERE!
Long time away from the games and kites—
HERE SLOBBERWACKY! COME OUT, COME OUT, WHEREVER YOU ARE!
So rested he by the Duff billboard, and grumbled loudly...
CLEAN UP AFTER YOUR PETS, YA JERK!
SURLY SEZ: THE NEXT MILE OF SPRINGFIELD FOREST IS PROUDLY SPONSORED BY DUFF BEER
Duff
SURLY
THIS BITES!

And as in selfish thought Bart sat, the Slobberwack, with eyes ablaze,
Came staggering through the Springfield woods,
And burping as it came!
AYE CARUMBA!
AAHHOOOOOOO! BURP
Plink, Plunk! Plink, Plunk! Hitting head and trunk!
SURLY
TAKE THAT! AND THAT! AND THAT!
ARROOOO! OW! ARROOOO! OW!
The slingshot sang! The Wack did stumble!
OOOOOH!
Bart knocked it out,
HEH, HEH, HEH! BARTHOLOMEW J. SIMPSON-1; UGLY MONSTER-0!
Then gave a shout...
YAAAAHH!!

STORY	PENCILS	INKS	LETTERS	COLORS	EDITS	JABBERWOCKY
JESSE LEON MCCANN	JAMES LLOYD	TIM BAVINGTON	KAREN BATES	NATHAN KANE	BILL MORRISON	MATT GROENING